BUCKNELL REVIEW

Making History: Textuality and the Forms of Eighteenth-Century Culture

STATEMENT OF POLICY

BUCKNELL REVIEW is a scholarly interdisciplinary journal. Each issue is devoted to a major theme or movement in the humanities or sciences, or to two or three closely related topics. The editors invite heterodox, orthodox, and speculative ideas and welcome manuscripts from any enterprising scholar in the humanities and sciences.

This journal is a member of the Conference of Editors of Learned Journals

BUCKNELL REVIEW
A Scholarly Journal of Letters, Arts, and Sciences

Editor
PAULINE FLETCHER

Associate Editor
DOROTHY L. BAUMWOLL

Assistant Editor
STEVEN W. STYERS

Contributors should send manuscripts with a self-addressed stamped envelope to the Editor, Bucknell University, Lewisburg, PA, 17837.

BUCKNELL REVIEW

Making History: Textuality and the Forms of Eighteenth-Century Culture

Edited by
GREG CLINGHAM

Lewisburg
Bucknell University Press
London and Toronto: Associated University Presses

Associated University Presses
440 Forsgate Drive
Cranbury, NJ 08512

Associated University Presses
16 Barter Street
London WC1A 2AH, England

Associated University Presses
P.O. Box 338, Port Credit
Mississauga, Ontario
Canada L5G 4L8

The paper used in this publication meets the
requirements of the American National Standard for
Permanence of Paper for Printed Library Materials Z39.48-1984.

(Volume XLII, Number 1)

ISBN 0-8387-5384-1
ISSN 0007-2869

1001873154

PRINTED IN THE UNITED STATES OF AMERICA

Contents

Recent Issues of BUCKNELL REVIEW

The Senses of Stanley Cavell
John Cage at Seventy-Five
Comedias del Siglo de Oro and Shakespeare
Mappings of the Biblical Terrain: The Bible as Text
The Philosophy of John William Miller
Culture and Education in Victorian England
Classics and Cinema
Reconfiguring the Renaissance: Essays in Critical Materialism
Wordsworth in Context
Turning the Century: Feminist Theory in the 1990s
Black/White Writing: Essays on South African Literature
Worldviews and Ecology
Irishness and (Post)Modernism
*Anthropology and the German Enlightenment: Perspectives on
    Humanity*
*Having Our Way: Women Rewriting Tradition in Twentieth-Century
    America*
Self-Conscious Art: A Tribute to John W. Kronik
Sound and Light: La Monte Young/Marian Zazeela
Perspectives on Contemporary Spanish American Theatre
Reviewing Orpheus: Essays on the Cinema and Art of Jean Cocteau
Questioning History: The Postmodern Turn to the Eighteenth Century

Notes on Contributors

STEVEN BLAKEMORE, associate professor of English, Florida Atlantic University, is the author of *Burke and the Fall of Language* (1988) and two books (*Intertextual War* and *Crisis in Representation*) on the revolutionary debate in the 1790s.

GREG CLINGHAM holds the National Endowment for the Humanities Chair in the Humanities at Bucknell University, where he is also the director of the University Press. Among his publications are *Boswell: The Life of Johnson* (1992), the edited *New Light on Boswell* (1991), the co-authored *Literary Transmission and Authority: Dryden and Other Writers* (1993), the edited *Cambridge Companion to Samuel Johnson* (1997), the edited companion volume to *Making History—Questioning History: The Postmodern Turn to the Eighteenth Century* (*Bucknell Review* 41: 2 [1997])—and the forthcoming *Writing Memory: Textuality, Authority, and Johnson's "Lives of the Poets."*

ADRIANA CRACIUN, assistant professor of English at Loyola University, Chicago, has published articles on Mary Lamb and Charlotte Dacre and edited Charlotte Dacre's novel *Zofloya* (1997). She is currently co-editing, with Kari Lokke, *British Women Writers and the French Revolution.*

MADELEINE KAHN is the author of *Narrative Transvestism: Rhetoric and Gender in the Eighteenth-Century English Novel* (1991) and of articles on various eighteenth-century topics. She teaches at Mills College, Oakland, California, and is at work on a book about teaching at a women's college.

ERIN F. LABBIE, who was a participant in the Dartmouth School of Criticism and Theory (1995), has published articles on Boswell and on the medieval "Lombarda Tenson." She is a doctoral candidate at the University of Minnesota, where her dissertation blends psychoanalytical theory with metafictional analysis of medieval and eighteenth-century literature.

Lisa Naomi Mulman is a doctoral student and instructor in English at Duke University, where she is working on her dissertation, entitled "Rituals of Imagination: The Catholic Aesthetic in the Modern American Novel."

Martin Wechselblatt is associate professor of English at the University of Cincinnati and the author of *Bad Behavior: Samuel Johnson and Modern Cultural Authority* (1998).

Introduction:
History between Text and World

THE essays in *Making History* continue a discussion of the general theme of the earlier, companion volume, *Questioning History*.[1] This theme is about the nature of reference in eighteenth-century texts and the relation between discourse and truth, or between fiction and history, in writing about the real, the social and political, and the personal. A central question is asked by Cathy Caruth: "How can we think of a referential—or historical, or material—dimension of texts that is not simply opposed to their potentially fictive powers? How might the very fictional power of texts be, not a hindrance to, but a means of gaining access to their referential force?"[2]

The paradoxical relationship and tension between the referential (understood usually as a truth-effect) and the fictive (understood as the necessary use of rhetoric and the tropological) in historical texts has been at the center of recent philosophical and theoretical considerations of historiography. Roger Chartier has drawn attention to the dangers inherent in the identification of historical discourse with narrative and historical truth with discourse. Although past reality might be accessible only through texts, as Chartier and many other historians recognize, this is not the same as "postulating that the logocentric and hermeneutic logic governing the production of discourse is identical to the practical logic ruling conduct and actions. All historical stances must take into account that experience is not reducible to discourse, and all need to guard against unconstrained use of the category of the 'text.'"[3] Chartier's concern lest the realm of the material and the practical be absorbed into that of the discursive and the textual in historiography is directed at what he (and others) see as the complete relativity of Hayden White's privileging of tropes and language in historical narrative.[4] Such relativism, Chartier argues, "disarms" history which then "loses all capacity to choose between the true and the false, to tell what happened, and to denounce falsifications and forgers."[5]

9

Although this particular idea of history does not by any means represent the totality of Chartier's thought about historical discourse, it does formulate a problem faced by historiographers wishing to bridge (or account for) the gap between the past and its representation. Chartier's language suggests that truth and falsehood and the historical event itself are clearly defined and self-evident categories and that they somehow preexist the historical discourse that registers their existence. At the same time, Chartier's terms seem to imply that it is the business of responsible historiography to police those boundaries and that gap between the true and the false, between the historical event and the pseudohistorical event, because they might otherwise be easily and dangerously distorted when history permits itself to be tainted by discourse or textuality.

In the context of eighteenth-century studies that "gap"—and attempts to police or to bridge it—is particularly problematic for a variety of related reasons. Because the Enlightenment has been identified in postmodern culture as the origin of modernity itself (with all the categorical restrictions from which postmodernism has tried to escape), we have had much invested in maintaining a rigid concept of Enlightenment institutions and practices.[6] But even as we have recognized and explored the linguistic sophistication and self-consciousness of eighteenth-century texts, and positioned them more thoroughly within the contexts of postmodern and new historical readings of eighteenth-century culture, our conception of the historiography of eighteenth-century culture has not kept pace. To recognize, in eighteenth-century texts, the performativity of language in the production of historical knowledge—whatever generic form that knowledge might take—is to blur the boundaries between genres, to pose fundamental questions about the nature of personal and social identities, and to undermine the notion of the eighteenth century as an origin for anything modern. As Martin Wechselblatt suggests in his essay on "The Canonical Ossian," to call into question the established, empirical, and dichotomous ways of conceptualizing history (as Macpherson does in his forged translations) is also to undermine (and to begin to remake) the canon as established in the eighteenth century, and to confront the "emergence of canonicity as a system of textualized social relations."

In the case of both Macpherson (as discussed by Wechselblatt) and Chatterton (as discussed by Greg Clingham) it becomes clear that the status of their work as forgery is inseparable from their status as historical discourse and critique. In both cases, the specific historical interventions that are represented by Macpherson's *Ossian* and Chatterton's Rowley poems bring into question the idea of a canon and the idea of the nation on which it is based, even while the eighteenth-century writers themselves participate in producing a commensurate nationalist ideology. While both Macpherson and Chatterton employ a deliberately fictionalized historical narrative to write in and to make alternative imagined national communities from the ones in which they find themselves, Clingham uses Peter Ackroyd's novel *Chatterton* as a postmodern reflection or echo of Chatterton's own practices in the forgeries and argues that Chatterton's conception of history is iterative. Paradoxically, Chatterton's historical narrative (as reflected in Ackroyd's text) reveals history as being *at once* empty—as being (in the words of Paul Ricoeur) the mark of a trace of something that had passed this way[7]—*and* also deeply and materially engaged in the production of social and personal realities.

This ambiguity—of history and historical discourse being *at once* textual *and thereby* materially engaged and productive of new historical realities—governs all the essays in this volume, and it informs their sustained exploration of that difficult gap between historical truth and fictional discourse.

For Madeleine Kahn and Steven Blakemore that historical critique takes the form of a kind of binary and (in the deconstructive terms enunciated by J. Hillis Miller)[8] even parasitic intertextual relationship between two or more texts that opens up a space for the making of an alternative history. Blakemore argues that the revolutionary discourse of writers like James Mackintosh in the 1790s was produced through the imitation and appropriation of an earlier set of terms about discovery and enlightenment by writers like Bacon and Locke. Of importance here is the recognition that both conservative and revolutionary sides in the 1790s are fighting previous ideological battles about authority and innovation in political life, and both resort to a similar enlightened terminology from the past to develop their different rhetorical purposes. Blakemore notes that both opponents and advocates in England of the French Revolution "wrote in and out of the same system of representation," telling different stories of the historical past, according to their respective political dispositions, but nonetheless complementing each other in a peculiar intertextual palimpsest.

For Madeleine Kahn the relationship between Ann Yearsley's poem "To the Honourable H___E W___E" (1784) (reproduced in an appendix to her essay) and Horace Walpole's *The Castle of Otranto* (1765) is also palimpsistic, but here the act of textual appropriation that goes into making Yearsley's alternate reading of Walpole has specific class and gender connotations. The laboring-class Yearsley develops a persona in the poem that adopts the voice of Walpole's Bianca, a female servant. In so doing Yearsley generates a critique of the political and patriarchal organization and values of Walpole's Gothic tale. Yearsley certainly admires and praises Walpole's tale; yet her act of locating Walpole as a kind of literary origin, whose cultural authority authorizes her own writing, turns out to be an act of reinscription that makes marginal perspectives more central to the tale. Crucially, for Kahn, Yearsley's political position in the poem is developed as part of a historical narrative and reiteration, since her poem's dialogic relationship with *Otranto* enables Yearsley to develop and change elements in the tale itself. This procedure is precisely in keeping with the translated yet fictional aspect of the novella. Offering itself as a "translation" of a (pseudo and invented) sixteenth-century text which had itself supposedly been written three hundred years before, *The Castle of Otranto* embraces fiction to make its present historical point, and, indeed, to make history. Yearsley's poem nicely plays into and echoes Walpole's historiographical problematics.

This performativity of historical discourse likewise governs the three other essays in this volume in different, yet significant, ways for rethinking the polymorphous nature of historical thinking in the eighteenth century. Lisa Mulman discusses, in implicit Lacanian terms, the ways in which material objects (the rosary, the veil) become laden with desire in Matthew Lewis's *The Monk*. This novel interrogates the discursive relation of material objects to each other and to personal perception (especially sight), and, as Mulman remarks, goes beyond the nominal Freudian dichotomy of inside-outside to invest objects with an erotic dimension and to make sexuality the site for revelation of the objective. This investment, then, is the cutting edge for a critique of religious, especially Catholic, sensibility, but it also recognizes the power of objects to transform the self. Just as Antonia's veil is ambiguous, at once that which hides and reveals, and that which signifies chastity and stimulates desire, so Ambrosio's behavior is not the expression of the repressed inner self, but rather the outer self in an act of textual performance.

Performativity explicitly encompasses both self and history in Erin Labbie's discussion of the idea of *retro* as metaphor for historical narrative in Charlotte Lennox's *The Female Quixote*. Drawing on the work of Kaja Silverman, Luce Irigaray, Diana Fuss, and Mary Ann Doane, Labbie argues that Lennox uses Arabella's cross-historical dressing as a multidimensional textual device that effects the novel's conceptualization of both the feminine gender and of the history within which women perform, and which they themselves make. Arabella's retro dressing enables the crossing of the vestimentary boundaries of the midcentury bourgeois culture, as well as an evasion of the commodifying gaze of men, thereby articulating the identity and the desire of woman, and making it inassimilable by the conventional division of the novel's discourse into romance, novelistic fiction, and history. At the same time, Arabella's cross-historical dressing constitutes a powerful alternative historiography: it does not merely attempt to erase the difference between past and present, as the doctor attempts to persuade her, but it develops a theory of history as "reiteration and recreation": "she draws on fictional history to create her own present, therefore rendering that which has been marginalized as 'fictional,' true for her in the present. By engaging in retro dressing, Arabella enacts the reality of the fiction she lives."

Arabella's retro dressing (as do the forgeries of Macpherson and Chatterton, themselves a kind of "trying-on" of past guises) has a violent effect on her community, suggesting not only the conservative and patriarchal nature of mideighteenth-century society, but also the institutional pressures operating to maintain a conception of history where fact and fiction are clearly identified and remain in the hands of those in a position of cultural power. In the final essay of this volume, Adriana Craciun considers the impact of literal violence by women in the French Revolution on the feminist cultural discourse of Mary Wollstonecraft, Mary Robinson, Catherine Macaulay, Helen Maria Williams, and others in the 1790s. Although these writers of the 1790s adopt a variety of ambiguous attitudes toward the morally fraught question of violent women, and the difficult negotiations around bodily strength in the relationships between men and women, Craciun demonstrates how the issue enabled Wollstonecraft, Robinson, and others to articulate fundamental questions about the cultural construction and permeability of the female body, and the dynamics of social and sexual power integral to that process, that became central to feminism and feminist critiques of Western history in the twentieth century. Although Wollstonecraft did not share or anticipate in any obvious way Foucault's idea (in *Discipline and Punish*) that the soul is the prison of the body, Craciun demonstrates that she (and others of her decade) had a clear sense of the female body as ideological construct, and they urged women to adopt various personal, sexual, dietary, domestic, and political practices that could support alternative historical explanations for the relations between the sexes so that, in turn, those historical explanations would help change material circumstances.

Foucault's argument, in *The Order of Things,* that the late eighteenth century saw a shift in epistemic organization from the classical, in which language and objects coexisted within the realm of representation, to the modern, in which the "historical" was born in the separation of the sign from the signifier (and language exceeded the limits of representation), is a complex one that has been absorbed into a wide range of interpretations of eighteenth-century literate culture and its modernity.[9] The essays in *Making History* and the earlier *Questioning History* have, in their own ways, subscribed to the notion of that general cultural shift in the eighteenth century, and to the concomitant recognition that the eighteenth century is, in certain fundamental ways, continuous with (though obviously not identical to) the postmodern. Acknowledging that the postmodernism of the late twentieth century sees itself and sees the obverse of itself in the cultural movements of the eighteenth century does not necessarily entail the uncritical recuperation of the shibboleths of the Enlightenment, although it does require us to become more skeptical of our own. Each of the essays in these two volumes identifies discursive practices in a wide range of eighteenth-century texts that stand in a skeptical, dialectical relation to the dominant linguistic, philosophical, and cultural systems of the day, very much in the way Nick Groom and Charlie Blake describe the historical operation of forgery, a quintessential postmodern turn: forgery is "a literary plot— a narrative—that mimics the metanarratives of scholarship and history and ventriloquizes history"; forgery is thus the reinvention of the past, a plot—a discourse—in which "the text is not dehistoricized, but history is made iterable."[10] Very much in the mode of Dominick LaCapra's historiographical situating of the "text" and "criticism" between history and literature,[11] different from yet dialectically partaking of both, the essays in *Questioning History* and *Making History* exemplify an openness to the material life outside the generic autonomy of narrowly defined genres. They thus register the typical interdisciplinary way eighteenth-century texts *make* history in the act of *questioning* history and bridge the gap between the past and its representation in the present that Roger Chartier poses as a central historical problem. The eighteenth century is one place in which we understand that the historical event is, paradoxically, always intimately dependent on historical discourse.

GREG CLINGHAM

Notes

1. See *Bucknell Review* 41 : 2 (1997), ed. Greg Clingham, *Questioning History: The Postmodern Turn to the Eighteenth Century.*

2. Cathy Caruth, "Introduction: The Insistence of Reference," in *Critical Encounters: Reference and Responsibility in Deconstructive Writing,* ed. Cathy Caruth and Deborah Esch (New Brunswick: Rutgers University Press, 1995), 2. See also Cathy Caruth, *Unclaimed Experience: Trauma, Narrative, and History* (Baltimore: Johns Hopkins University Press, 1996), chap. 4, "The Falling Body and the Impact of Reference."

3. Roger Chartier, "History between Narrative and Knowledge," in *On the Edge of the Cliff: History, Language, and Practice,* trans. Lydia G. Cochrane (Baltimore: Johns Hopkins University Press, 1997), 19–20.

4. Ibid., 33–35.

5. Ibid., 34.

6. See Joan De Jean, *Ancients against Moderns: Culture Wars and the Making of a Fin de Siècle* (Chicago: University of Chicago Press, 1997), chap. 1, "Did the Seventeenth Century Create Our Fin de Siècle? or, The Making of the Enlightenment That We May at Last Be Leaving Behind."

7. Paul Ricoeur, *Time and Narrative,* 3 vols. (Chicago: University of Chicago Press, 1984–88), 3 (1988), trans. Kathleen Blamey and David Pellauer, 119.

8. J. Hillis Miller, "The Critic as Host," in *Deconstruction as Criticism,* ed. Geoffrey Hartman (New York: Continuum, 1987), 217–54.

9. For a useful presentation of Foucault's complex argument in *The Order of Things,* see Michael Payne, *Reading Knowledge: An Introduction to Barthes, Foucault, and Althusser* (Oxford: Blackwell, 1997), chap. 4.

10. Nick Groom with Charlie Blake, "Introduction," *Narratives of Forgery,* ed. Nick Groom, *Angelaki* 1, no. 2 (Winter 1993–94): 6.

11. Dominick LaCapra, *History and Criticism* (Ithaca: Cornell University Press, 1985) and *Rethinking Intellectual History: Texts, Contexts, Language* (Ithaca: Cornell University Press, 1983). See also Suzanne Gearhart, "History as Criticism: The Dialogue of History and Literature," *Diacritics* 17 (1987): 56–65.

BUCKNELL REVIEW

Making History: Textuality and the Forms of Eighteenth-Century Culture

The Canonical Ossian

Martin Wechselblatt
University of Cincinnati

> For just who were the British? Did they even exist?
> —Linda Colley, *Britons: Forging the Nation, 1707–1837*

FOR the traditional literary historian, history revealed itself in the shape of canons. This was, of course, to overlook the historical contingency, the modernity, of canonicity. Contemporary literary history has distinguished itself by turning its attention to the social processes by which canons are formed. In the pages that follow I will be asking what form history takes when it manifests itself canonically, in the peculiar language of canonicity. As a beginning into the many issues such a project raises I will take as my main example those most canonical of noncanonical texts, Macpherson's Ossian poems.

Most often, the historicity of canons makes itself felt as it reveals itself in the forms of a crisis in community values, usually in the sense of a revelation of otherness within a community. To judge only from the mass media's current silence on the topic after a decade of near hysteria, the most recent culture wars have drawn to a close. One result has been the publication by significant houses of some new anthologies, the bread and butter of academic publishing. Now in print is the *Norton Anthology of Afro-American Literature,* joining the *Norton Anthology of Literature by Women.* Due for publication in 1998 is a two-volume *Anthology of British Literature* from Longman which places literary and nonliterary texts in dialogue with each other, and is aimed at capturing the market held for so long by *The Norton Anthology of British Literature.* These and other publications testify to the gradual institutionalization, over the last few years, of changes in ideas of canon formation that were not so long ago the causes of acrimonious debate and institutional crisis. To appreciate how fully academia has emerged from the culture wars one must read *Bright College Years: Inside the American Campus Today,* the recent book by Anne Matthews. Matthews herself is a journalist who contributed a memorable share to the media's projection of academia's fall from its humanist mandate—in particular, an article in *The New York Times Magazine* featuring a photo of Andrew Ross in a pumpkin colored sport jacket by Comme il Garcon, a sartorial statement that was to become the emblem of academia's self-serving, fashion-mongering, insularity and arrogance. Reading Matthews's new book, however, one would never know the culture wars had even occurred. When she writes that "the first task of a campus is the advancement of knowledge for its own sake," she is no longer lamenting the betrayal by "liberals" of an until now universally acknowledged principle of Western civilization. Far from it: she is describing what she regards as the actual condition of contemporary higher education, both in principle and in fact. Matthews illustrates the currency of this principle through numerous anecdotes involving socially awkward but intellectually honest faculty who work hard to realize what she describes as the university's tripartite purpose: "Scientists scout the future's edge, social scientists make sense of the present, humanists are professional rememberers."[1]

Matthews divides the disciplines into a set of clichés: the scientist as romantic pioneer, eyes on the future; the sociologist as pragmatic sense-maker, concerned with the here-and-now; the humanist as repository of shared cultural memory, guarding against the depredations of time. Nonetheless, it is worth noting that the humanist is the only one of the three to be qualified as a "professional." This is interesting for us because the first humanists to operate in what we understand today as a "professional" context were in fact journalists, the "news-writers" of whom Samuel Johnson famously complained that they can "confidently tell today what [they] intend to contradict tommorow," or "affirm fearlessly what [they] know they will be obliged to recant," and are therefore certainly no respecters of cultural memory.[2] Today we might say that journalism emerged in the eighteenth century as a literary form which, along with the novel, expressed in its formal features the discontinuous experience of secular, modern, historical time. And by the same token, we might also see the emergence of the concept of "professionalism" as an attempt to reimagine and in a manner salvage the traditional forms of cultural authority in the face of this experience of discontinuity and historical disconnection. So it is appropriate, though highly ironic, that a journalist reminds modern (academic) humanists that they are (also) professionals. However, this is, as it turns out, doubly ironic, in that by doing so Matthews also implicitly calls into question the very possibility of the sort of historical conservation—and the neatly parcelled out divisions between past, present, and future—to which her reminder was intended to lend credence.

Before turning to my peculiar case of canonicity, Macpherson's Ossian poems, I want to take as my starting point a paper by Ross Chambers entitled "Irony and the Canon," delivered at the Modern Language Association's annual meeting in 1988 and published soon afterward in *Profession*. The argument here is very much that of an "insider," which Chambers himself in fact argues all teachers of literature are, and what they are "inside" of, moreover, is a canon—it doesn't matter which one. "[T]he problem of opposition," Chambers writes, "is always how to combat what has made us what we are . . . [and thus] always involves a degree of struggle against oneself."[3] In addition to its obvious Oedipal overtones, such a formulation resonates through a number of contemporary discourse theories, historicist and deconstructive alike, which focus on the "embeddedness" of identity within its conditions of possibility—theories concerned with the formation of subjectivity, the relationship dialectical or otherwise, between identity and its conditions of possibility, between consciousness and its (variously figured) determinations. What all such approaches generally share is a commitment to an immanent, internal critique of discursive or material structures from within themselves. Thus they also inevitably tend to reflect on the grounds of their own critical enterprises. The theme of *authorship*, in particular, has offered the opportunity for critics to reflect on their own discourse even as they analyze the conditions of possibility informing or governing the writings of others similarly defined. So, for Chambers, the issue is not "the products of the canon"—which books are included and which not. Rather it is the structure or "system of canonicity" itself which must be thought through and addressed by teachers and critics. Otherwise, he warns, our critical discourse will suffer from a "blindness to its own constitution and function within the system it works against."[4] Even Michel Foucault, writing of the immanent disappearance of "the author," was nonetheless clear that *some other* aspect of print culture would always be exercising the "author function":

It would be pure romanticism, however, to imagine a culture in which the fictive would operate in an absolutely free state, in which fiction would be put at the disposal of everyone and would develop without passing through something like a necessary or constraining figure.[5]

What is appealing about irony in this context is how plain it makes the fact that discourse "can only be produced relationally," thus foregrounding the irreducibly mediated condition of *all* intentionality:

> I can intend irony as much as I like, but it has not worked unless and until it has been perceived—"read into" my discourse by another. . . . On the other hand, once it has been perceived, it exists independently of my intention. . . . And between the intended irony that goes unperceived, and the unintended that becomes irony by being perceived, there is room for many kinds and degrees of misunderstanding, misfire, and fizzle, as well as understanding and complicity.[6]

Still, irony comes in but two forms for Chambers. In the first place, it may be merely "negation"—as when a person asserts their superiority over some element or other of their culture from which they wish to distance themselves. M. Homais's ironic remark about kitsch in *Madame Bovary* serves as an example. Nothing is so conventionally bourgeois, Homais fails to realize because he is so deeply bourgeois himself, as detesting kitsch, and his ironic disparagement only ends by affirming the system of values he opposes. To this Chambers contrasts an irony he calls "appropriative"—that is, an irony which openly displays the ambiguity of its implication for the system of values it gestures outside of without ultimately escaping. Recent work on Swift's irony, for instance, has made very strong claims for it in these terms, particularly in regard to his misogynistic representations of women.[7]

However, one could speculate that Chambers's two versions of irony—indifferent as they are to the great variety of ironic gestures—actually signify two versions of textuality. The first, Chambers's "negation," says one thing but means another. The second, "appropriative irony," says two things and means them both—hence its implicit assertion that it cannot escape the "relational" or binary construction of the given discourse within which it occurs and which is its fundamental condition of possibility. Considered as modes of signification, the first implies a hermeneutic, surface/depth model of discourse, in which one meaning is deeper, and thus more authentic, than the other. The second implies a structure of undecidability, which confronts us with both the need to choose and the impossibility of doing so. Choice, as one critic describes it in another context, becomes the occasion for exercising an already made choice.[8] That is, readers choose on the basis of a hierarchy of values already in place within themselves. Both text and reader are thus revealed to be complicit in a larger system of relations, one which renders the reader's values highly visible by foregrounding both the act of choosing and the occasion for the choice.

But if irony renders text and reader complicity in the reproduction of a given discourse, it does not render them simply identical. "I can intend irony as much as I like, but it has not worked unless and until it has been perceived—"read into" my discourse—by another. . . . On the other hand, once it has been perceived, it exists independently of my intention." The authority with which the reader's choice is made both derives from the text and does not, can at one moment appear *a reading* and at another *a being read*. Irony in this sense illuminates an aporia between agency and representation, function and meaning, whose alternation, Jane Tompkins has argued in a widely influential study, characterizes the history of Western European criticism.[9] It is within this aporia that "Ossian" is situated.

I

For a number of reasons, the well-known controversy over Macpherson's self-described translations of ancient Highland poetry marks simultaneously the first major challenge to and emergence of canonicity as a system of textualized social relations. For one thing, it makes no sense to speak of a canon of English literature before the second half of the eighteenth century. The concept did not exist because the institutions responsible for it did not exist. This is changed radically in the aftermath of the Reformation and then especially the universal vernacularizing thrust of print capitalism—with its increasingly sophisticated systems of production and distribution: subscription replacing patronage, stables of anonymous writers working for hire, the advancing of advertising and promotional techniques, as well as the spread of provincial booksellers and the innovation of lending libraries. In the most practical of its senses, canonicity refers to the organization of a particular type of mass-produced commodity (a vernacular commodity) for consumption. As it happens, books were in fact the very first mass-produced commodities; and the first best-selling author, "the first writer who could 'sell' his new books on the basis of his name," was perhaps Martin Luther.[10]

The debate over the authenticity of the poems bearing the name "Ossian" was carried on, and is frequently still carried on, in unremittingly nationalist terms; and canons are nationalist projects—perhaps the essential, self-confirming nationalist project: establishing the continuity of a given vernacular culture with (a very different social formation) the political history of a given nation-state.

> Here it is useful to remember that the universality of Latin in medieval Western Europe never corresponded to a universal political system. The contrast with imperial China, where the reach of the Mandarinal bureaucracy and of painted characters largely coincided, is instructive. In effect, the political fragmentation of Western Europe after the collapse of the Western Empire meant that no sovereign could monopolize Latin and make it his-and-only-his language-of-state, and thus Latin's religious authority never had a true political analogue.[11]

Nationalism replaces participation in the imagined community of Christendom when vernacular and state languages coincide and are given dramatically new fixity by print capitalism in a form capable of seemingly infinite reproduction, temporally and spatially. Certain dialects and literary forms were, of course, closer to each print language and thus achieved greater prestige within the national culture.

The social function of traditional bardic poetry had to do with legitimizing the perogatives of a few dominant families, not with affirming a feeling of national community. Until, that is, the Ossian controversy chaneled the animosity of the recently suppressed Highlands into the powerful idea of a national culture. On the English side, an important issue was whether these translations provided access to an original *British* culture prior to the Norman invasions—the "Norman Yoke" deplored by Whigs and Tories alternately.[12] Authorized by a universalist historiography which placed all cultures on a single time line from "primitive" to "civilized," the equation of England with ancient Britain suppressed their historical difference by annexing the latter as a "primitive" version of the former.[13] Virtually authorized by the union of the crowns in 1707, this sort of cultural appropriation was even more urgently felt in the decades following the suppression of the clans in 1745. Like all "inventions of tradition," canon formation among them, the cultural absorbtion of the Highlands proceeded through a reciprocal series of inclusions and exclusions. The elimination of certain symbolically charged artifacts, such as the tartan, completed the '45's belated military and economic enforcement of the Act of Union. At the same time, ancient Scottish poetry was being "recovered" south of the border for a history of British literature culminating in and establishing a genealogy for the "native genius" of something very like *greater England.*

The Scots themselves, however, were similarly employed upon the project of discovering a national culture—though not necessarily a British one. Arguing with both zeal and precision that Ossian was "the collective product of the Scottish Enlightenment," Richard Sher has demonstrated that "Macpherson, it is true, produced the Ossianic 'translations' themselves, but the Edinburgh 'Cabal' provided the inspiration, incentive, financial support, letters of introduction, editorial assistance, publishing connections, and emotional encouragement that brought Ossian into print."[14] It may have been the author of *Douglas* (1756), John Home, who was the first to suggest to Macpherson that he attempt some translations from the Gaelic. In any case, it was Home who brought Macpherson's first efforts to the attention of notables in Edinburgh. Two of the most notable of these were the political economist and clan member Adam Ferguson and The Reverend Hugh Blair, the latter writing to David Hume that Macpherson had practically to be "entreated and dragged" into the work by his new friends.[15] Ossian's fortunes would be joined forever after to Blair's through his *Critical Dissertation on the Poems of Ossian, Son of Fingal*—from 1765 the definitive guide to the poems for readers in Scotland, England, and, very soon, the Continent. It was Blair's emphasis on, not the warlike but the sublime and sentimental aspects of Ossian's warriors, which set the tone for Macpherson's reception among German readers and scholars, so crucial for the subsequent development of modern philology, ethnography, and the study of folklore. Blair testified that Macpherson's Gaelic material had been collected "under my eye," but at least one modern scholar has suggested that Blair's participation "may have gone appreciably beyond that of a midwife."[16] Both he and Macpherson alike did exceedingly well as a result of their mutual association with "Ossian." Though Blair's own name was regarded highly enough by 1765 to confer considerable authority on Macpherson's alter ego, from the 1770s Blair's sermons became bestsellers and his *Lectures on Rhetoric and Belles Lettres* (1783) perhaps the most frequently consulted of English treatises on "taste," particularly in translation abroad.

Nor was the influence of Scottish Enlightenment figures such as Blair and Ferguson confined to practical matters of production and distribution. In his exhaustively (many have said obsessively) annotated 1805 edition of Macpherson's works, Malcolm Laing demonstrated the degree to which the sublimity, sentiment, and sympathetic imagination of Ossian's moral and aesthetic universe, celebrated by Blair, reflects the ideas of Thomas Reid among others of the Aberdeen philosophical set, where Macpherson went to college. Laing even argues that in the last volume of Ossian's poems, *Temora* (1763), Macpherson incorporates echoes of and allusions to works with which Blair compares *Fingal* in his *Critical Dissertation.* Such an array of circumstantial evidence, both internal and contextual, would have been more than enough to support among Englishmen Johnson's characterization of Ossian as a "Scotch conspiracy in national falsehood."[17]

Of perhaps equal circumstantial interest, at the very time Samuel Johnson was demanding to see Macpherson's original Gaelic manuscripts he was himself actively engaged in preparing the biographical and critical introductions for a major collection of English poetry. In fact, *The English Poets* was commissioned by a conger of London booksellers seeking to prevent the immanent publication of a Scottish edition from seizing control of the copyrights to these poems. Having achieved this end, the canonical status of this particular ensemble of poets was more or less guaranteed for decades to come through the authority Johnson's name lent to their company. As Boswell puts it in a letter to Johnson on first hearing of the project:

> Pray tell me about this edition of *"The English Poets,* with a Preface, biographical and critical, to each Authour, by Samuel Johnson, LL.D." which I see advertised. I am delighted with the prospect of it. Indeed I am happy to feel that I am capable of being so much delighted with literature. But is not the charm of this publication chiefly owing to the *magnum nomen* in the front of it?[18]

In characteristic fashion, Boswell expresses his delight at the literary project and then more delight at his capacity to be delighted by things literary. But as the following remark about Johnson's *"magnum nomen"* suggests, Boswell himself suspects that the delight readers feel with themselves because they are readers is not mediated through literature as such, but rather through the aura which attaches to the names of certain authors. (Even if he is merely flattering Johnson, he is doing so through a convention which implies just this.) It is the presence of Johnson's name on these volumes which enables them to function as the medium through which Boswell is enabled to feel good about being Boswell—in a manner which we, in turn, today recognize as particularly "Boswellian."

Now one aspect of the Ossian controversy which continued to perplex Macpherson's English critics was his inexplicable resistance to attaching his name to the poems. For it was universally agreed that, had he presented his poems as, say, imitations rather than translations, his genius would have been celebrated throughout the British Isles and his own "*magnum nomen*" sought out for further projects. Of course, it is precisely Macpherson's refusal to attach his own name to the poems which makes them forgeries, though refusal may not be the appropriate term here. According to at least one source, a man as reliable as any other in this matter, "when the reputation of the poems was fully established, he felt no objection to be considered as capable of composing such works himself." That is, once Macpherson had raised himself from Highland poverty through the connections and profit Ossian brought him, "his pride made him wish to believe, that he owed that elevation, more to his own talents, than to the genius of an old bard, whom he had rescued from oblivion."[19] One can admit a strong, even dominant, element of sheer personal calculation in Macpherson's motives and those of his Edinburgh allies, it seems to me, without imagining anything as banal and as conscious as Johnson's notion of a "conspiracy." Instead, we need to consider the various dimensions of the Ossian controversy as expressing a concert of often contradictory and not always conscious interests which, in playing themselves out, maneuver between and articulate some of the structural possibilities for questioning cultural legitimacy in this period. However personally calculated and encouraged by others similarly motivated, Macpherson's naming of his work reveals much about the contemporary zeal for inventing national literary traditions, on both the English and Scottish sides of the border.

Indeed, in the next phase of his career, Macpherson's talents proved as effective when they were placed at the service of England's political interests in India as they had shown themselves to be serving Scotland's cultural prestige everywhere else. While collecting material for his first volume, the *Fragments,* Macpherson became acquainted with a certain Dr. John Macpherson, of Sleat, who would remain one of his most useful sources of Highland lore through *Temora* and the growing controversy. But it was his friendship with Dr. Macpherson's son, also John, which would open up a new and even more lucrative career as a colonial operative in Tanjore and propogandist for the governments of North and Pitt. It was John who first established contacts with the court of the Nabob of Tanjore in 1767, which he then grossly exaggerated in London as an appointment to negotiate in the Nabob's name. It seems he assisted his claims in this impersonation by producing a document with an impressive seal written in a language no one could read. George McElroy has described in painstaking detail the intricate weave of misrepresentations, frauds, and lies that the two Macphersons spun out over the next fifteen years for the benefit of the Ministry, frequently playing Westminster off against Madras for their own greater enrichment.[20] It was during this period that James Macpherson, already famous as the translator of Ossian, was to add to that the admiration of Warren Hastings, who thought him "one of the only two men he could call 'wise.'"[21] It is also during this period that we find James Macpherson engaged in forgeries which he is most certainly not calling translations. His 1775 *History of Great Britain* was probably written by Alexander Dow, a close friend of James and John. (McElroy suspects the manuscript may have been payment for arranging Dow a lucrative posting in Bengal.)[22] More valuable to Westminster was his extraordinary *History and Management of the East-India Company* (1779), an imaginative representation of Company dealings with local princes that supported Ministerial allegations in Parliament. This time, Macpherson's text recasts an already existing written history, Orme's *History of the Military Transaction of the British Empire in Indostan,* to which the translator of Ossian turns the familiar repertory of his stylistic techniques and documentary devices, including references either too broad to track down with certainty, footnoted to multiple sources, or drawn from "private information" "in the hands of the author."

II

The central generic preoccupation of English literary nationalism was the repeatedly aborted or failed attempts of English writers over the long eighteenth century to produce a national epic of compelling power. Milton and Dryden planned Arthuriads, Pope a Brutiad, but none were ever composed. Blackmore's *Prince Arthur* (1695), *King Arthur* (1697), and *King Alfred* (1723) managed to make it to press, but found no readership. Each attempted to appropriate the aura of a prior culture, Saxon or Roman, for the genealogical prestige of the contemporary English. Each seeks the image of England in the mirror of a prior *locus imperium.* "Dryden," Michael McKeon writes, "was fascinated by this idea of the revolution in time which gives birth to a new age simultaneously old, and he used every means he could think of to express it adequately."[23] Dryden's *Aeneid* and Pope's Homer translate the ancients into the idiom and verse of contemporary England and thus, bearing the revivifying power of a *translatio imperii,* these projects could be said to reproduce, on the level of poetic form, Aeneas's smuggling of his household gods into Latium—the founding of Rome as the second Troy.

Macpherson's Scottish *Fingal* (1762), on the other hand, is arguably the only successful, original national epic of the entire period. And it, ironically, was passed off as a translation. It is this irony I want to consider.

We should note that it was not the poem's artistic merit (which was widely acknowledged), but the question of its authenticity—which is to say, its historical status—that compromised *Fingal*'s success even as it brought the work notoriety. Unlike Dryden and Pope, Macpherson was indifferent to the problem of reproducing ancient versification, and thus unlike their translations, his was done into prose. Instead of discussing the problems of versification in his introductory material, Macpherson dwelt on the issue of historicity. The preface he appended to his earlier publication, *Fragments of Ancient Poetry* (1760), is in two parts: one an exercise which attempts to establish the dating of the poems, and another arguing that these poems are actually the surviving fragments of a unified epic. The latter does not merely introduce the notion of a formal unity, but, more I think to Macpherson's point, the impression of a historical unity—of an entire and until now unsuspected historical era which awaits recovery. Macpherson does indeed recover it himself two years later with the publication of *Fingal.* Amazingly, in his *Critical Dissertation* Blair argues that the historical authenticity of the epic was demonstrated precisely because Macpherson's prose made not the smallest pretense of formal connection to his original:

> Elegant, however, and masterly as Mr. Macpherson's translation is, we must never forget, whilst we read it, that we are putting the merit of the original to a severe test. For we are examining a poet stripped of his native dress: divested of the harmony of his own numbers. . . . If, then, destitute of this advantage, exhibited in a literal version, Ossian still has power to please as a poet . . . we may safely infer, that his productions are the offspring of true and uncommon genius.[24]

To concentrate for a moment on Blair's figure of the undressed Highlander, it seems that while English authorities were busy stripping the Highlander of such symbolic dress as the tartan in order to make him safely "British," Macpherson was at work exposing the Highlander's "true" figure, so to speak, beneath the figures clothing him.[25] While Englishmen were busy annexing Scottish history as an ancient province of England's own, *Fingal* was deploying similar tactics to uncover an era out of English reach. The irony here, the "appropriative irony" (to return to Chambers's phrase) is that Macpherson did this in English, the very language of the cultural translation he was resisting. Indeed, many of the antique poems Macpherson drew on for his own were dialogues between Oisin and Saint Patrick, in which each seeks to overmaster the other's culture in displays of rhetorical skill. Macpherson in turn took a scene of confrontation between opposing cultures, and refigured it as an antagonism internal to a single cultural project: England's *British* myth.

It is within this context that the thematics of the proper name in *Fingal* itself becomes clear, reflecting back on Macpherson's refusal to put his name to it as author. Ossian is the son of Fingal and father of Oscar. Both Fingal and Oscar die before him, leaving Ossian, as he laments, isolated on an island of history cut off from past and future. Yet it is not Ossian who is actually thus isolated, not the historically invested character who goes by this name in the poem, but rather more exactly the bardic "voice" through which this poem imagines history being fashioned:

> Roll on, you dark-brown years. . . . Let the tomb open to Ossian, for his strength has failed. The sons of song have gone to rest. My voice remains, like a blast, that roars, lonely, on a sea-surrounded rock, after the winds are laid. (*PO*, 1:297)

The character "Ossian" descends into the tomb, while his "voice" remains behind—divested, to be sure, of its place in a historical series, dehistoricized and "disembedded," but for all that still available for appropriation, recontextualization, reinsertion into another historical series. This, it seems to me, is just what Macpherson was up to in reworking, forging, or, in his term, translating the Oisin poems. The "voice" Of "Ossian" is the figure of the "true" Highlander which Hugh Blair thought Macpherson's "literal version" uncovers beneath the "dress" of Gaelic versification. Nonetheless, that "voice" is also itself merely a figure, capable of historical reinscription and of movement across eras. Ulti-

mately, the profound sense of loss which this "voice" expresses is neither only that which properly belongs to a previous era, nor only that which is attached to the events of 1745. Rather, as the name for a constellation of historical significance, 1745 marks the moment at which the continual depredations of the past are viewed as the loss of a national culture. It names clan losses as national losses, retrospectively inaugurating the historical moment of a Scottish national culture at the same point its impossibility is acknowledged. Thus the date, 1745, functions like the proper name "Ossian" to mark the translation (Macpherson's term) of a figure across eras, from a temporally isolated and irrecoverable past into a present which recovers that past in its own image. However, unlike the specular recoveries and translations of Pope and Dryden, "Ossian" recovers the past in the image of a present loss, as the simultaneous immanence and impossibility of nationhood. In short, *the nation as forgery,* and not just the Scottish nation. For the proper name "Ossian" marks the translation of Gaelic culture into England's national myth of Britain. The "voice" is no longer that of Oisin, who confronted the invader toe-to-toe, but of an Oisin reborn in the image of the invader, who speaks from within him, in the invader's own language.

As Peter Murphy argues, Macpherson's forgeries transformed the "mystery" of the Highlands, the sheer lack of knowledge about them, into a "mystery" of another order—a marketable cultural commodity.[26] But even so, Ossian speaks the language of commodification against itself by revealing the mythologizing function of the project to which his poems owe their existence as much as Scotland owes the immanent yet impossible idea of its nationhood. The paradox is captured in the mute, uninscribed stone witness Ossian erects to the future:

> [I]n memory of the past . . . I took a stone from the stream, amidst the song of bards. . . . Prone, from the stormy night, the traveller shall lay him, by thy side: thy whistling moss shall sound in his dreams: the years that are past shall return. Battles rise before him, blue shielded kings descend to war. . . . He shall burst, with morning, from dreams, and see the tombs of warriors round. He shall ask about the stone; and the aged shall reply, "This grey stone was raised by Ossian, a chief of other years! (*PO,* 2:355)

The stone's origin recalls the "sea-surrounded rock" emblematic of Ossian's temporal isolation. It too represents the idea of a historical era, but, uninscribed, it tells no story, cannot situate itself within a particular series of events on its own. Those events occur elsewhere: in the dreams of the traveler, for which the stone provides the merely formal occasion, and in the recollections of the "aged." But as Ian Haywood points out, what is remembered by these living witnesses is nothing more nor less than "the *act* of remembering" itself—Ossian's raising of the stone "in memory of the past." Significantly, no characteristic editorial footnote directs us at this point to some actually existing stone. The monument "remains an imaginary transmitter of history."[27] Just as what living memory remembers is the act of remembering, so the historicity Macpherson insists upon for his translations derives from nothing, neither more nor less, than the act of producing them itself. In Austin's sense of the term, Macpherson's recovered epic displays the performative nature of national memory.

Peter Murphy's critique of the poems as examples of Scotland's cultural commodification tells, therefore, only part of the story. Macpherson's poems demystify their commodity form just as they do the nationalism of British literary history, from within, by replacing the "mystery" of their referent with the "mystery" of their production. To put it another way, they displace questions of representation and meaning through the performance of their occasion and function.

As Hugh Kenner memorably observes in a similar context, the counterfeiter "imitates not things but occasions," "not a visible thing but an invisible event."[28] Ossian counterfeits a moment of historical origin, of emergence into time, and the consequent spatialization of time in the form of an artifact. *Fingal's* dream stone represents this "invisible event"—a tautology, since "events" are, after all, by definition temporal, not spatial—as the act by which the things of history are introduced into history, and time is reified. It is from such "invisible events" that "not the canon, but the system of canonicity" is derived. What Chambers calls "the products of the canon" are such "imaginary transmitters of history" as the proper name "Ossian," the *magnum nomen* "Samuel Johnson, LL.D.," or as Ossian's stone, which recalls nothing more or less than its own foundation—though it serves, perhaps for that very reason, as the occasion for the traveler's encounter with history as both immanent and dreamlike.

Notes

1. Anne Matthews, *Bright College Years: Inside the American Campus Today* (New York: Simon & Schuster, 1997), 15.

2. *Idler* 30, in Samuel Johnson, *Selected Essays from the "Rambler," "Adventurer," and "Idler,"* ed. W. J. Bate (New Haven: Yale University Press, 1969), 289.

3. Ross Chambers, "Irony and the Canon," *Profession 90* (New York: PMLA, 1990), 18.

4. Ibid., 20.

5. Michel Foucault, "What Is an Author?" in *Textual Strategies: Perspectives in Post-Structuralist Criticism,* ed. Josue V. Harari (Ithaca: Cornell University Press, 1979), 159.

6. Chambers, "Irony and the Canon," 19.

7. See, for two well-known examples, Ellen Pollak, *The Poetics of Sexual Myth: Gender and Ideology in the Verse of Swift and Pope* (Chicago: University of Chicago Press, 1985), chap. 6 and Laura Brown, *Ends of Empire: Women and Ideology in Early Eighteenth-Century English Literature* (Ithaca: Cornell University Press, 1993), chap. 6.

8. Fredric Bogel, unpublished ms., "The Rules of the Game." I am grateful to Professor Bogel for permission to cite his unpublished ms.

9. Jane Tompkins, "The Reader in History: The Changing Shape of Literary Response" in *Reader-Response Criticism: From Formalism to Post-Structurlism,* ed. Jane Tompkins (Baltimore: Johns Hopkins University Press, 1980), esp. 205–6.

10. Benedict Anderson, *Imagined Communities: Reflections on the Origin and Spread of Nationalism,* rev. ed. (London: New Left Books/Verso, 1991), 39.

11. Ibid., 41.

12. For a succinct summary of the "Norman Yoke's" history as a political football in the eighteenth century, see Earl Wasserman, *The Subtler Language: Critical Readings of Neoclassical and Romantic Poems* (Baltimore: Johns Hopkins University Press, 1959), 113–16. A fuller account of the political climate can be found in H. T. Dickinson, *Liberty and Property: Political Ideology in Eighteenth-Century Britain* (London: Weidenfeld & Nicolson, 1977), chap. 2.

13. Johannes Fabian, *Time and the Other: How Anthropology Makes Its Objects* (New York: Columbia University Press, 1983), 11–36, 97–104.

14. Richard Sher, *Church and University in the Scottish Enlightenment* (Edinburgh: Edinburgh University Press, 1985), 254.

15. John Hill Burton, *Life and Correspondence of David Hume* (Edinburgh, 1846), 1:406.

16. Howard Gaskill, "'Ossian' at Home and Abroad," *Strathclyde Modern Language Studies* 8 (1988): 13.

17. James Boswell, *Life of Samuel Johnson,* ed. Pat Rogers (Oxford: Oxford University Press, 1980).

18. Ibid., 800.

19. Sir John Sinclair, *A Dissertation on the Authenticity of the Poems of Ossian* (London, 1808), xiii.

20. George McElroy, "Ossianic Imagination and the History of India: James and John Macpherson as Propagandists and Intriguers," in *Aberdeen and the Enlightenment,* ed. J. S. Carter and Joan Pittock (Aberdeen: Aberdeen University Press, 1987), 363–74.

21. Ibid., 366, quoting Hastings to John Macpherson, 27 January 1784.

22. Ibid., 372, n.11.

23. Michael McKeon, *Politics and Poetry in Restoration England: The Case of Dryden's "Annus Mirabilis"* (Cambridge: Harvard University Press, 1975), 264.

24. James MacPherson, *Poems of Ossian,* 2 vols. (London, 1806), 1:132; hereafter *PO,* cited in the text.

25. The wearing of tartan was confined, significantly, to Highland regiments serving with the British army. Though determined to destroy Highland ancestral values, the traditional obedience and bravery of Scotsmen serving their clans in battle was thought highly desirable if placed under the command of Whitehall. See Linda Colley, *Britons: Forging the Nation, 1707–1837* (New Haven: Yale University Press, 1992), 119–20. As it happens, it

was precisely the civic, or republican virtue of Scottish clansmen, rising to serve their laird in time of need, that appealed to Adam Ferguson about Macpherson's Gaels. Ironically, for Ferguson this civic virtue represented a necessary corrective to commercialism with its effeminate love of luxury and acceptance of despotism; but the freedom allowed the tartan solely within the British army, the appropriation of the civic virtue it could be seen to represent, was one step in a primarily commercial process of pacification.

26. Peter T. Murphy, "Fool's Gold: The Highland Treasures of MacPherson's Ossian," *ELH* (1986): 567–91.

27. Ian Haywood, "The Making of History: Historiography and Literary Forgery in the Eighteenth Century," *Literature and History* 9 (1983): 147.

28. Hugh Kenner, *The Counterfeiters: An Historical Comedy* (New York: Anchor/Double-day, 1973), 89, 73.

Chatterton, Ackroyd, and the Fiction of Eighteenth-Century Historiography

Greg Clingham

Bucknell University

The relation between fiction and history is assuredly more complex than we will ever be able to put into words.[1]

I

THE relations between fiction and history have become increasingly important in contemporary historiography as well as in rethinking literary and historical genres in the eighteenth century. In discussing the referential function of language, Cathy Caruth draws on Paul de Man's attempts to distinguish reference from natural law as a way of preventing history from being swallowed up by the abstract power of language: paradoxically, "direct or phenomenal reference to the world means . . . the production of a fiction" precisely because reference is radically different from natural law.[2] For Linda Hutcheon, a similar paradox governs postmodernism: "The past really did exist, but we can only know it today through its textual traces, its often complex and indirect representations in the present."[3] In the post-Foucaultian world the linguistic basis of personal, social, and historical realities has become a commonplace, pointing to the argument that there is no stable, clearly accessible, or transcendental ground of truth in the human and social sciences. Richard Rorty, Jean-Françoise Lyotard, Michel Foucault, and other cultural philosophers have uncovered the fictional nature of master narratives in the human discourses. Yet the general deconstruction of British and American historical and literary practices has tended to draw a line on this side of the Enlightenment. While many individual

35

writers, whole genres, and certain social and cultural phenomena in the eighteenth century have been subject to revisionist critical treatment, the eighteenth century is still deemed in its central intellectual identities to be wedded to an instrumental and enlightened reason and to the naturalistic transparency of the language that authorizes it.

Thomas Chatterton, however, is one figure who has more readily lent himself to a recognition of the liminal and reflexive nature of mideighteenth-century attitudes. While Chatterton was once considered as marginal in literary history—as being significant more for being erected by English romantic writers into a symbol of the quintessential poetic spirit—the transformation of the eighteenth-century canon has placed Chatterton's work in a new light. Crucial to the historiography of Chatterton's writing is its status as forgery. Discussions of Chatterton's activities have traditionally focused on the socioeconomic, moral, and literary aspects of his forgeries, rather than on their historiographical form and identity. Recently it has been suggested that two particular developments determined the public receptivity of forgery in mideighteenth-century England: (1) the copyright act of 1709 enforced "the notion of art as intellectual property owned by an individual originator," thus confirming the separation of forgery from the overtones of artistic creativity which it had in the Renaissance and turning forgeries into "subversive artefacts";[4] and (2) developments in capitalist economy commodified notions of historiographical truth, making manuscripts (and other objects of art) the bearers of information as well as valorizing them as material objects, that could be seen and touched, that could sustain an eyewitness account, and that could be placed in a museum.[5] These two discourses are closely linked. While Ben Jonson could compliment Shakespeare unequivocally for his capacity to forge, meaning his poetic creativity,[6] by the 1760s forgery of the kind practiced by Horace Walpole in *The Castle of Otranto*, James Macpherson in *The Works of Ossian*, and Thomas Chatterton in the Rowley poems and various other texts, was seen as a conspiracy to undermine the centers of institutional authority.

Yet the material and paternal conception of artistic property that identified forgery as subversive of cultural and historical authority also veiled an insight into the profoundly binary and textual nature of history that a writer like Chatterton was to uncover in his forgeries. As Nick Groom notes, in the hands of Chatterton forgery is not only a plot against the law and the fathers of cultural authority, it is a "literary plot—a narrative—that mimics the metanarratives of scholarship and history and ventriloquizes history,"[7] thereby indicating a binary relationship between forger and the original authors and texts. "Original" texts and forgeries of those texts are an integral part of the same cultural system and mode of production. Forgery is a reinvention of the past, a plot in which "the text is not dehistoricized, but history is made iterable."[8] Certainly, Chatterton attempts to ventriloquize both historical and paternal authority in his invention of alternate historical origins for the city of Bristol, and of the moral idealism of the fifteenth-century Sir William Canynge in the pseudo-medieval *Bridge Narrative*, *Bristowe Tragedy*, and other Rowley documents involving the historical but fictionalized Canynge.[9] Chatterton invents and invokes the "medieval" voice of Thomas Rowley in order to compose a body of literature (poetry, drama, historical documents, letters, medical and architectural treatises) that endowed the eighteenth-century mercantile city of Bristol with a history of artistic sensibility, devotion, heroism, and nobility. Accompanying the fabricated literary documents were designs of heraldic crests, ancient coins and pedigrees, and drawings of the churches, bridges, gateways, and statuary that were supposed to represent the glories of the medieval city of Bristol.[10] All of these had supposedly been created by the imaginary poet-priest Thomas Rowley for the merchant prince Sir William Canynge, a historical figure who had actually been mayor of Bristol five times in the fifteenth century. Significantly, according to Rowley's legend, Canynge had donated the money acquired from his slave trade and merchant empire to artistic enterprises of various kinds, but especially to the rebuilding of St. Mary Redcliffe church, where Chatterton's father had discovered the parchments.

Thus Rowley (as Chatterton's poetic voice) gave Chatterton a leverage on the past and enabled him to engage a number of different needs and interests at once. While those interests involved a redefinition of the notion of the unity and clearly defined identity of the poetic self, they implied an interest in defining the notion of a secular nation out of the remnants of a religious medieval, monarchical past. As Benedict Anderson has argued vis-à-vis the creation of the secular concept of the nation in the eighteenth century, Chatterton's interest in reimaging the community of Bristol also emphasized the function of print, of printing and textuality in the process of making and authenticating history.[11] Furthermore, as Nick Groom observes, Chatterton's enterprise demanded the fixity of print

> because forgery, as a narrative of becoming or of being printed, is a story with an end: the story seeks closure, which is the acceptance

of the forgery in a decontextualized printed state. The press is this instrument of textual authority. Print delimits a space in which meanings of authenticity—or meaning generally—might work.[12]

Similarly, Susan Stewart connects the material process by which Chatterton attempted to authenticate (that is, to "antiquate" and then to print) the Rowley documents with his desire to *inscribe* the law of the father: "Chatterton is not taking part in an Oedipal scene where he would supplant the Father, nor is he simply legitimating him, so much as attempting to fill the absence of his authority." "But," Stewart continues, "because there is no referent here, we have a great deal of authority with very little authenticity."[13] It is this "inauthenticity" that troubled Horace Walpole when, in 1769, Chatterton offered him *The Ryse of Peyncteyne, yn Englande, wroten bie T. Rowlie, 1469 for Mastre Canynge* to supplement his own *Anecdotes of Painting in England* (1762).[14] Initially impressed by what *The Ryse of Peyncteyne* seemed to offer him, Walpole asked to see more of the work of the Thomas Rowley whose views and poetry were represented in the manuscript, with a view to publishing some of them under the Strawberry Hill imprint.[15] But the prospect of print made Chatterton careless and hasty; he sent the much less convincing *Historie of Payncters yn Englande bie T. Rowley,* accompanied by a scarcely veiled plea for patronage, and Walpole's suspicions of this material were confirmed by Gray and Mason. He declined to promote or to publish Chatterton and advised him to mend his ways. The precise terms of Walpole's rejection are interesting. As he wrote in 1778:

> though I had no doubt of his [Chatterton's] impositions, such a spirit of poetry breathed in his coinage . . . : nor was it a grave crime in a young bard to have forged false notes of hand that were to pass current only in the parish of Parnassus. . . . I told him also, that I had communicated his transcripts to much better judges, and that they were by no means satisfied with the authenticity of his supposed MSS.[16]

Forgery, it appears, does not cancel out the "spirit of poetry," yet Walpole's economic metaphor ("forged false notes of hand") is used to block Chatterton's entrance into Parnassus, and this leads to branding the manuscripts as inauthentic. "Poetry" clearly escapes the censure of inauthenticity because the question of authenticity refers to the materiality of the pseudo-medieval manuscripts and to the historical view that they imply and authorize. In other words, Walpole's response to Chatterton registers his

resistance to the iterability of history, because *that* "plot" deessenti-
alizes the notion of historical originality, of historical origin, and
the line of teleological and temporal development that sustains
that cultural narrative.[17]

Haywood remarks that in the Walpole affair "Chatterton could
not reveal his creation to be the modern recreation of history that
it was. Rather, it had to be the original history, the ancient artefact.
Behind the forgeries, lay the judgment of Johnson on Ossian: 'As
a modern production, it is nothing.'"[18] I am arguing, however,
that it is precisely as a "modern production" that Chatterton's
texts draw attention to, and signify, their status as historical documents. In their seemingly gratuitous textuality and their "inauthentic" claim to reflect the real world of the past, Chatterton's
forgeries raise the question of what history is, and they thereby
figure their own historicality. It is not quite, as Susan Stewart suggests, that the absence of a referent in the forgeries undercuts
their historical content on the basis that to be historical a text
needed to be authentic.. It is rather, as Cathy Caruth argues, that
"the recognition that direct or phenomenal reference to the world
means, paradoxically, the production of a fiction."[19] That fiction,
however inauthentic (when measured by empirical and traditionally positivistic standards of historical realism), is what gives access
to history.

II

To propose fiction as necessarily incident to history in Chatterton's texts is to identify them as postmodern. Postmodern and
eighteenth-century texts share a number of historiographical
principles: first is that historical understanding is a provisional,
contradictory enterprise working skeptically within established
forms of epistemological, literary, and historical authority; second
is that the historian's language is aware of its own relativity, even
its emptiness, even while it constitutes its own meanings, and that
there is no privileged point of view from which to make judg-
ments; and third that history makes its specifically historical
meanings through narrative, specifically through the telling of
stories. Underlying these principles is the knowledge that the relationship between text and historical "truth" partakes of a kind of
double reading, in which the language of the text (its textuality)
both inhabits and deconstructs the metaphysical structure (the
historical truths and events) it records. Forgery partakes of such

a double reading, according to Groom and Blake, for "[F]orgery is a literary plot—a narrative—that mimicks the metanarratives of scholarship and history."[20]

As several critics have already argued, postmodern fiction (or metafiction) provides us with an eloquent opportunity for considering the continuities and discontinuities between Enlightenment and postmodern texts.[21] According to Linda Hutcheon, postmodern fiction "is a formal manifestation of both a desire to close the gap between past and present of the reader and a desire to rewrite the past in a new context,"[22] and formally it is therefore very like an eighteenth-century work. In what follows, I wish to argue that Ackroyd's novel *Chatterton*[23] "repeats" and reinscribes the life and work of Thomas Chatterton, and thereby draws attention to the historicality that characterizes Thomas Chatterton's eighteenth-century forgeries of the fifteenth-century Thomas Rowley. But this historicality is itself paradoxical, because its essence—paradoxically both "eighteenth century" and postmodern—lies in its particular kind of nothingness ("As a modern production, it is nothing"). This nothingness, however, is the echo or sign of a textuality that recognizes and repeatedly marks the movement of historical time. As Paul Ricoeur notes, history records the past passage, the trace, of something having happened, yet "the vestige or mark 'indicates' the pastness of the passage, the earlier occurrence of the streak, the groove, without 'showing' or bringing to appearance 'what' passed this way."[24] For Ricoeur, this is what history is: "To say that it is a knowledge by traces is to appeal, in the final analysis, to the significance of a passed past that nevertheless remains preserved in its vestiges."[25] What I therefore wish to propose is that Chatterton's texts are historical in responding to and recreating the trace of historical time, and that Ackroyd's novel conceptualizes the difference between then and now—repeats and defers the closure of history as a metaphysical system—by holding up a mirror to that trace and allowing us to see it more fully in operation.

Peter Ackroyd's *Chatterton* exemplifies ways in which fiction functions to produce historical knowledge—not just the "postmodern" knowledge of the novel, but the "eighteenth-century" knowledge of Chatterton's forgeries. But whereas the novel's irony suggests pastiche—a self-conscious manipulation of stylistic features that keep the text within its own terms—I suggest that the novel's ventriloquization engages with and unveils actual eighteenth-century practices. Although Hutcheon argues for the political and therefore the historical engagement of postmodern

parody, "a value-problematizing de-naturalizing form of acknowledging the history . . . of representations," I wish to explore how
the novel operates on a principle of alterity, how its self-
consciousness has as its teleology contact with a *real* eighteenth-
century past, even though that past is itself elastic, and, in a sense,
empty, and even though that past can be known only "through its
textual traces."[26] Ackroyd's text is also, in a similar sense, empty.
But although this problematizes his text, separating its repre-
sentiveness from any hegemonic concept of historical truth, it
does not prevent its textuality from becoming an index of its
representative function, contrary to the emphasis on the self-
referential aspect of language in the discussions of history writing
by Hayden White and Linda Hutcheon.[27] Neither does the idea
of Chatterton's and Ackroyd's textuality *necessarily* reinstate the
old opposition between literary or philosophical "text" and historical "narrative," as Nancy Armstrong and Leonard Tennenhouse argue happens in postmodern theory.[28] But following
Caruth's and de Man's argument about the fictionality of truly
representative writing, *Chatterton's* referentiality adds a cutting
edge (one even wants to say, a *substance*) to postmodern historiographical theory as a practical, revelatory (and therefore historical) means of reading eighteenth-century texts, and even proposes
that it might be most current in its preoccupations by being most
like eighteenth-century practice. By noticing what Ackroyd does
with history, we might reconceptualize the ideological power of
Chatterton's project—his forgeries as well as his death.

Ackroyd's novel consists of three narratives featuring different
historical moments and individuals: the 1760s of Chatterton; the
1850s of the poet George Meredith, his wife Mary Ellen Meredith,
and the painter Henry Wallis; and literary London of the 1980s
in which we meet an assortment of poets, novelists, librarians,
artists, art critics, art dealers, and art forgers. Each of the three
narratives tells its own story: the eighteenth-century story is about
Chatterton's life, death, and work; the nineteenth-century story
is about the creation in 1855 of a famous painting (now in the
Tate Gallery) of Chatterton on his death bed by Henry Wallis,
and also about the relationship between George Meredith (who
models for Wallis), and his wife Mary Ellen. The contemporary
story has several plots, the main one of which involves the well-
meaning but failed poet Charles Wychwood. Charles finds a (fake)
portrait of Chatterton as a middle-aged man dated 1802 and
identified as being by one George Stead; he is given some sensa-
tional (forged) manuscripts by a (fictitious) descendent of Chat-

terton's (fictitious) posthumous publisher Samuel Joynson,[29] which engenders Charles's interest in Chatterton and his "discovery" that the eighteenth-century poet had faked his own suicide in order secretly to write or imitate (or forge) many of the great poems now attributed to Gray, Goldsmith, Dyer, Cowper, and Blake. All of this is, of course, a joke on Ackroyd's part, but one with a serious import, for in the course of the narrative Charles comes to understand Chatterton's forgeries—both the actual eighteenth-century texts as well as the additional fantasized forgeries that Ackroyd weaves into the historical record—as essentially literary and as giving him access to the *real* world, of both past and present, in a way nothing else does.[30]

> When he awoke he noticed that the leaves had been swept away, and a young man was standing beside him. He had red hair, brushed back. He was gazing intently at Charles . . . [Charles] stretched out, yawning, and in that movement it was as if the clay had fallen away from his limbs; the strangeness had left him. . . . Then he walked through the gate. (*C*, 47)

Supporting the Wychwood story are other lesser plots making playful and ironic references to the connections between forgery, plagiarism, and "original" literature, suggesting that Ackroyd wants us to keep in mind the question of the boundary, and its erasure, between fiction and history, and between different historical epochs. For example, the novelist Harriet Scrope is discovered to have plagiarized the plot of a novel from a forgotten Victorian writer, and Stewart Merk, administrative assistant and executor to the painter Joseph Seymour, turns out to have forged Seymour's later works. Both of these plots draw attention to the economic and social basis of artistic value in identifying how the public would react to the news of the less than authentic work of the two artists involved. Real as the material considerations are, in both cases the characters—and the novel itself—accept the ironic fact that the artistic quality of the works in question is not really undermined by the knowledge of their "inauthenticity."

Charles's obsessiveness is comically portrayed; his sightings of the ghost of Chatterton are perhaps a temperamental quirk or a symptom of his constitutional headaches. But the novel never becomes, nor is the reader permitted to feel, superior to Charles's folly: the other characters (including George Meredith) also glimpse the ghostly young man with the red hair (see *C*, 70, 73, 166); and the "nineteenth-century" narrative shows us the poet

Meredith and the painter Henry Wallis both having their lives shaped by their recollected and imagined contact with Chatterton. Moreover, Charles's visions finally seem to have a *real* effect upon him. His last vision, occurring at the time of his collapse in an Indian restaurant, is a moment of real honesty: Charles defends the meaningfulness of poetry in the face of his friends' cynicism, expresses a rare tenderness toward his wife, and acknowledges his inadequacy as a husband and as a poet:

> "Of course words survive. How else could Chatterton's forgeries become real poetry?" He paused again, rubbing his hand slowly across his forehead. "And there are lines so beautiful that everything is changed by them." (*C*, 151)

> "I'll tell you what it is. It is a dream of wholeness, and of beauty. All the yearning and all the unhappiness and all the sickness can be taken away by that vision. And the vision is real. I know. I've seen it . . . ." He turned towards her [his wife] and smiled. "I'm sorry, love," he said. "I'm sorry you were stuck with me. I tried my best but it wasn't good enough, was it?" (*C*, 152)

Later, in the hospital, Charles wakes up in the eighteenth century, and dies in a physical posture uncannily reminiscent of the posture of Chatterton on his death bed, as modeled by George Meredith and painted by Henry Wallis. In a transparent but compelling passage of the novel, Charles is fully conscious of himself, but *feeling* as if he were acting a part, dying someone else's death:

> Charles reached down with his right hand and touched the bare wooden floor; he could feel the grain of the wood, and with his fingers he traced the contours of the boards. . . . At that instant of recognition he smiled: nothing was really lost and yet this was the last time he would ever see [his wife and his son], the last time, the last time, the last time, the last time. Vivien. Edward. I met them on a journey somewhere. We were travelling together. . . . His right arm fell away and his hand trailed upon the ground, the fingers clenched tightly together; his head slumped to the right also, so that it was about to slide off the hospital bed. (*C*, 168–70)

III

What larger narrative arises from this trope of collapsing one temporal scheme into another? Structurally, each of the "historical" narratives in the novel is discrete, in that each adheres to its own temporal scheme, plot, and stylistic features. In the novel, the characters Chatterton, Meredith, and Wychwood all sound like convincingly articulated and ventriloquized characters who reflect some real aspects of English life in the mideighteenth, the midnineteenth, and the late twentieth centuries respectively. But read as a commentary on the death of the historical Thomas Chatterton, the whole text traces and enacts a process of historical inscription as one historical person after another constructs his or her own version of the event. The end of the novel presents Chatterton's poisoning not as a suicide but as an accident (chapters 13–15)—he's trying to cure himself of gonorrhea by taking a mixture of arsenic and opium, and he miscalculates the dosage: "now, what were the proportions Dan gave me? . . . Was it one grain of arsenic for each ounce of laudanum? Or four grains?" (*C*, 224).

In choosing to develop his narrative in this way Ackroyd clearly chooses one series of "facts" out of a variety of contending theories about Chatterton's death, including the theory that it may have been accidental.[31] He disregards the historical record, as it has generally been taken to be, that Chatterton died wilfully by his own hand, a "fact" that has invariably been the starting and determining point for subsequent stories of his death and of its historical meaning. However, in drawing attention to Ackroyd's fictional narrative here I am not suggesting that his main intention is to offer an alternative historical explanation for the death of Chatterton, although the events as Ackroyd depicts them are historically plausible, internally consistent, and imaginatively convincing. But Ackroyd's invention is, in a sense, more telling than such an alternative biographical speculation, for it draws attention to the metaleptic process by which historical (and biographical) narratives and, therefore, historical (and biographical) truths are made and formalized.[32] Furthermore, Ackroyd's plot momentarily makes the death poignant and pathetic in unexpected ways, materially and pointedly contrasting it with the aesthetic *beauty* of the death as rendered in Wallis's painting (see below),[33] and questioning the romantic mythologization of the death as the tragic and sublime gesture of the archetypical poetic spirit.

Taken in the context of other knowledge of Chatterton, Ackroyd's narrative is self-consciously iterative; it is the most recent instance of a series of "historical" representations of the event, whose reality is unquestioned but whose meaning is narratively configured again and again in different ways. The novel does *not* offer from within its imaginative worlds any privileged perspective on these (or other) events—in fact, there are no observers in the book, not even Charles's son, Edward, although *his* conviction that his dead father lives on in the forms and in the spirit of the Wallis painting, is an innocent and charming one, and continues the compelling Renaissance theme in the novel that poets communicate with and possess each other across space and time. If we expect a historical account of a past reality to provide us with a definitive truth, as historical testimony this novel frustrates our desire of seeing what has really happened "beneath" the layers of cultural activity and textuality, just as the various paintings featured in the novel frustrate any attempt to find any definitive truth beneath the layers of paint.

But, as suggested, this novel's textuality is inseparable from "what has really happened," and its playfulness does *not* mean that the novel empties the notion of historical truth of meaning, although the truth that is offered by this text may be that history is empty. For its textual parodies and ventriloquizations, while questioning the authority of historical documents and the unity of artistic works and personal identity, invite a double reading that the text itself enacts upon history.

Such a double reading clearly happens in the relation of the three historical discourses to one another. Though distinct, those three temporal narratives are not actually successive: they are interwoven with each other, and the temporal progression of the whole book is unlinear; it starts in the twentieth century and ends in the eighteenth. Actually, the novel opens with a brief, encyclopedialike biographical entry for Chatterton, encapsulating the entire narrative in this concentrated, distanced, "historical" form (*C*, 1). Then the following pages (2–3) as well as the very last pages (233–34) of the novel frame the three sub- or mini-narratives, and are themselves placed in a kind of timelessness: pages 2–3 present fragmented (but important) insights representing each of the three temporal periods, and the closing pages have the three main characters—Chatterton, Meredith, and Wychwood—joining hands in a blaze of poetic afterlife ("Two others have joined him—the young man who passes him on the stairs and the young man who sits with bowed head by the fountain—and they stand silently beside him. I will live for ever, he tells them" [234]). These textual fragments it would seem make up a metanarrative about the *simultaneity* of different historical experiences and events. From such a point of view, it might be said that Ackroyd undoes the inexorable linearity of historical time so as to recuperate the eighteenth-century idea of a general

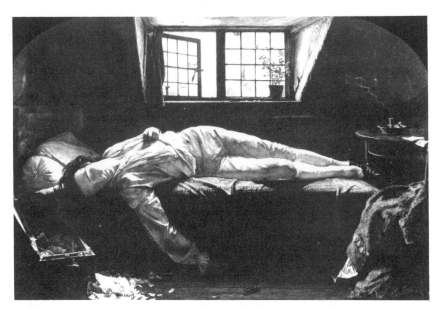

Henry Wallis, *Chatterton* (1856). By permission of the Tate Gallery, London/ Art Resource, New York.

human nature (as held by Dryden, Johnson, Burke, Wordsworth), and thereby to suggest the commonality of experience for Chatterton, Meredith, Wallis, Wychwood, and, presumably, the reader.

This reading of the structure of the novel is enabled by Wallis's 1855 painting of Chatterton on his death bed, a viewing of which (one imagines) may well have been the stimulus for Ackroyd's exploration of intertextuality and history in this novel. The painting was hung in the Royal Academy Exhibition of 1856, when John Ruskin praised it as "faultless and wonderful: a most noble example of the great school. Examine it well inch by inch, it is one of the pictures which intend, and accomplish, the entire placing before your eyes of an actual fact—and that a solemn one. Give it much time."[34]

Textually, the painting is itself, like the history in which Ackroyd places it, an empty sign that nonetheless brings together all significant elements and discourses of the text. The episode in which Wallis brings the painting to fruition opens up several important aspects of the novel, and is worth considering at some length:

On the following morning he began. . . . But as he watched that absolute white drying slowly on the canvas he could already see "Chat-

terton" as a final union of light and shadow: the dawn sky at the top
of the painting, softening down the light to a half-tint with the leaves
of the rose plant upturned to reflect its grey and pink tones; the body
of Chatterton in the middle of the painting, loaded with thicker colour to receive the impact of that light; and then a principal mass of
darkness running below. Wallis already knew that he would be using
Caput Mortuum or Mars Red for the coat of Chatterton, thrown
across the chair, and that he would need Tyrian Purple for the strong
colour of the breeches. But these powerful shades would stay in delicate contrast to the cool colours beside them—the grey blouse, the
pale yellow stockings, the white of the flesh and the pinkish white of
the sky. These cooler colours would then be revived by the warm
brown of the floor and the darker brown of the shadows across it;
and they, in turn, would be balanced by the subdued tints of the
early morning light. So everything moved towards the centre, towards
Thomas Chatterton. Here, at the still point of the composition, the
rich glow of the poet's clothes and the brightness of his hair would
be the emblem of a soul that had not yet left the body; that had not
yet fled, through the open window of the garret, into the cool distance
of the painted sky. (C, 164)

What strikes one first about this passage is the text's concentra-
tion upon paint—the materiality, the texture, the color of the
paint, and the literal forging of Wallis's procedure. Ruskin observes that "a *painter's* business is *to paint*, primarily; and that all
expression, and grouping, and conceiving, and what else goes to
constitute design, *are of less importance than colour, in a coloured
work.*"[35] Again, Ruskin notes of "the power of pure white light to
exhibit local colour" that "the expression of the strange, penetrat-
ing, deep, neutral light, . . . while it alters no colour, brings every
colour up to the highest possible pitch and key of pure harmoni-
ous intensity" (*LB*, 31).[36] Color, for Ruskin, is the key to composition: he might have been thinking of Wallis's painting when he
wrote that "if colour be right, there is nothing that it will not raise
and redeem" (*LB*, 52).[37]

Color, and the effect of light upon color, are clearly also the
terms in which Ackroyd imagines Wallis as making the painting
real, and making it germane to the historical dimension of the
composition. Wallis prepares, loads, and thickens the color to "receive" the light; and the light in the painted morning sky outside
the garret window will receive *and also resist* the soul of the dying
Chatterton: "a soul . . . that had *not yet* fled . . . into the cool distance of the painted sky." Ackroyd seems to understand Wallis's
use of color and light in the composition as (in Ruskin's words) a

kind of redemption, a vision of Chatterton *just* at the moment in which body and soul are parting—the "rich glow of the poet's clothes and the brightness of his hair would be the emblem of a soul that had *not yet* left the body."

"Redemption" here, however, is artificial; not only does the composition (in a manner reminiscent of Keats's Grecian Urn) generate an image of a complex, perpetually unfolding moment in time, "the entire placing before your eyes of an actual fact," as Ruskin says; but the composition also moves back on itself as composition, and collapses the idea of "Chatterton," his soul and his consciousness, into the pure materiality of paint:

> So everything moved towards the centre, towards Thomas Chatterton. Here, at the still point of the composition, the rich glow of the poet's clothes and the brightness of his hair would be the emblem of a soul that had not yet left the body.[38]

We are reminded here—not least by the echo of T. S. Eliot's meditation on the nature of time, history, and timelessness in the *Four Quartets*[39]—that the narrative of Charles's death (taking place "in" the twentieth century) is intersected by the narrative of Wallis's completion of the painting (taking place "in" the nineteenth century), which, in turn, represents an event "in" the eighteenth century. In chapters 10 and 11 of the novel, the focus changes frequently between modern and nineteenth-century scenes, and in ever shorter intervals of time they bring Charles-dying and Wallis-painting closer and closer to each other, until the two narratives become one. "Everything moved towards the centre."

Ackroyd's narratological move suggests a hypertextual connection and interweaving of Chatterton's existence in the portrait—that is, the moment of his death, before the soul had quite left the body—with Charles's death in the hospital. That coincidence of temporal moments is played out in many other little ways in the text. For example, Charles sees a vision of Chatterton lying on his death bed when he looks into George Stead's 1802 portrait; then, when looking at Wallis's painting, he sees himself lying in Chatterton's place, being mourned by his wife and son; at the same time, Charles's son, Edward, is convinced that Chatterton is still alive, because Wallis's Chatterton (who has the face of George Meredith) is different from Stead's Chatterton (*C*, 129–32). The curious recognition by Charles and Edward that Chatterton is "not dead yet" (132) is the moment at which the text first switches to a nineteenth-century perspective, and to Meredith modeling for Wallis in Chatterton's actual garret in Brooke Street, Holborn.[40]

If the superimposition of these scenes and events seems contrived, I suspect that was intentional and strategic on Ackroyd's part, a move designed to bring to mind a textual palimpsest or the layers of paint in the Wallis painting, but also in the fake Stead painting of 1802. An image of what lies "beneath" the Wallis painting (of *what* is represented by the artistic composition) is dramatically suggested by what happens to the Stead painting when the forger Merk tries to remove the layers of grime that hide the dim but essential forms underneath:

> With the varnish gone, the successive layers of paint became visible, and Merk could see the outline of some other object glimmering faintly behind the candle and the books. Inside the face of the sitter, too, another face could just barely be discerned; it was a younger face, and, as it seemed to Merk, one that expressed suffering.
>
> And then he cried out, in panic. The dissolvent was reacting with the freshly exposed paint. Small bubbles and creases were forming on the surface of the picture, and the image of the sitter seemed to shudder before beginning to shrivel, to bend, to drop away in flakes of paint. . . . The face of the sitter dissolved, becoming two faces, one old and one young . . . . Within a few minutes nothing remained: except, curiously enough, certain letters from the titles of the books which now hovered in an indeterminate space. (*C*, 228)

In Ackroyd's text, this moment of dissolution occurs at the same moment of the final dissolution, from arsenic and opium poisoning, of the eighteenth-century Chatterton:

> Chatterton is being tossed up and down upon the sodden bed, the agony rising from him like mist into the attic room. Hold on oh hold on until this fit is past but my hands are nailed to the bed, my flesh being torn from me as I curve and break. His face swelling, his eyelids bursting in the heat. I am the giant in the pantomime oh God save me from melting, melting, melting. (*C*,228–29).

IV

Ackroyd's (and Wallis's) multilayered artifice makes for a powerful representation of historical temporality.[41] Wallis's painting is one of the chief means by which Chatterton's end is known, and it reverberates throughout the novel just as it does through history.[42]

Since 1856, the "facts" of Chatterton's death, and even his place in literary history, have been influenced by the details and the impact of Wallis's painting. As Holman Hunt said: "The cruelty of the world towards poor Chatterton . . . will never henceforth be remembered without recognition of Henry Wallis, the painter who first so pathetically excited pity for his fate in his picture of the death of the hapless boy."[43]

Wallis knows, however, that "it was only through its fall into the world," that is, into temporality and history, "that [his vision] would acquire reality" (C, 164). That "reality" partakes of various overlapping forms, which, in closing, I would like to sum up briefly, and to suggest some other ways of pursuing the historical implications of Ackroyd's text and other metafictional texts like his.

Ackroyd's text is so structured as to articulate and to *inscribe* the notion of the iterability of history; it thereby demonstrates the essential place of fiction, especially narrative, in envisaging and constituting historical subjects and historical events. Both Paul Ricoeur and Hayden White write interestingly on how, in order to know what really happened in the past, the historian prefigures as possible objects of knowledge the whole set of events reported in "historical" documents.[44] From such a narratological point of view--largely applicable to both Ackroyd and Chatterton, as well as to other eighteenth-century writers—there is no significant difference between fictional and nonfictional narratives, and Chatterton's forgeries (as well as those of Macpherson and Percy) become a powerful form of history.[45]

Such a collocation between history and forgery, however, threatens the sense of cultural order and authority, because the plot of forgery undermines linear and unified conceptions of historical continuity, and because it points to the emptiness (but *not* the meaninglessness) of history as a sign. In his forgeries Chatterton pushes further than either Walpole or Macpherson the idea that an authentic-seeming history can be invented out of nothing (or out of fragments and traces of the past), and enforces the recognition that such a narratological procedure is no different from real, authentic history. Ackroyd understands this paradigm in Chatterton's texts and reiterates it in *Chatterton,* and so draws attention to the textuality of history that, nonetheless, generates a knowledge of that which has happened.

Unlike hegemonic or imperial views of history, which employ the resources of language positivistically to determine the truth-value and cultural acceptability of one particular set of truths and values, Chatterton's historiography (and Ackroyd's reiteration of it) suggests an alternative narrative for English history by uncoupling the historical from the authentic, and identifying history as "writing about the trace," about that which has past (and passed) and is known in the present by its textual traces. Hence, in the texts of both Chatterton and Ackroyd there is no relation of reproduction or equivalence between the narrative and the course of events that is being historically documented, but rather a metaphorical one. But that which is absent (past or passed) is not necessarily outside of memory (as it often seems to be in the linguistic work of Levinas and Derrida and in the historiographical work of White and Ricoeur). The narratological posture of Ackroyd toward Chatterton, and of Chatterton toward Rowley, is one of translation, exemplifying White's notion that "history is a mode of being-in-the-world that both makes possible understanding and invokes it as a condition of its own deconcealment . . . its method is hermeneutics, conceived less as decipherment that as 'interpretation,' literally 'translation,' a 'carrying over' of meanings from one discursive community to another."[46]

Translation, however, resists closure. Historiographic narrative as translation marks a move from what Walter Benjamin calls "Messianic time" to a culture-wide acceptance of "homogeneous, empty time," which Benedict Anderson associates with the process of imagining and writing the concept of the nation in the eighteenth century.[47] Translation is central to that process of nation-formation, as Homi Bhabha discusses in *The Location of Culture*.[48] Because of its doubleness--presenting itself as an act of repetition and at the same time as an act of interpretation that inscribes linguistic, cultural, and temporal difference—translation serves as a paradigm for the nation's constant negotiation between the particular and the universal. Because national identity is constructed, and there is no essential link between the individual's daily life and the perceived timelessness of the nation, national discourse always translates between the two. According to Bhabha, "the sign of translation continually tells, or 'tolls' the different times and spaces between cultural authority and its performative practices."[49] In discussing the liminality of the migrant experience within the context of strongly nationalist, centralized communities, Bhabha employs Benjamin's notion of the liminality of translation to define a particular kind of present that is reminiscent of the temporality I have been describing in Chatterton and Ackroyd:

This space of the translation of cultural difference *at the interstices* is infused with the Benjaminian temporality of the present which makes graphic a moment of translation, not merely the continuum of history; it is a strange stillness that defines the present in which the very *writing* of historical transformation becomes uncannily visible.[50]

Such temporality, is, in Anderson's words, an idea "in which simultaneity is, as it were, transverse, cross-time, marked not by prefiguring and fulfillment [a medieval conception that characterizes Messianic time], but by temporal coincidence, and measured by clock and calendar."[51] Narratologically, the emptiness and the temporal coincidence that marks modern conceptions of time has been identified by Frank Kermode as the content of narrative plot as such. Plot works

> to defeat the tendency of the interval between *tick* and *tock* to empty itself. . . . To put it another way, the interval must be purged of simple chronicity, of the emptiness of . . . humanly uninteresting successiveness. It is required to be a significant season, *kairos* poised between beginning and end. [Through plotting,] that which was conceived as simply successive becomes charged with past and future: what was *chronos* becomes *kairos*.[52]

However, as I have been discussing throughout, the historical narrative of Chatterton and of Ackroyd both raise questions of the emptiness of time and history, and both testify to the meaningfulness of the emptiness of historical narrative. As Sherman reads Kermode, "the new emptiness of time creates a need, a means, and a structure for fullness in text."[53] What creates and structures that meaningfulness, within emptiness, is (as Wallis is made to say by Ackroyd) the fall of the painting into the world, which is the literal fall of Thomas Chatterton. As Cathy Caruth explains when discussing Paul de Man's "The Resistance to Theory," falling registers the impact of the event, and "is thus the evocation of a referential reality neither fictionalized by direct reference nor formalized into a theoretical abstraction."[54] The reference, the historical edge, to Chatterton's forgeries and to Ackroyd's fiction thus emerges in the resistance of language to perceptual analogies. "So everything moved towards the centre, towards Thomas Chatterton."

The falling body of Thomas Chatterton appears in one narrative after another in Ackroyd's *Chatterton*, resisting assimilation even as it provides occasion for yet another narrated and historical event. Yet in its delayed resistance to the end and to closure, it marks not only how Chatterton has been historicized but also the historicality of his forgeries, and perhaps the movement of modern history itself.

Notes

1. Paul Ricoeur, *Time and Narrative*, 3 vols. (Chicago: University of Chicago Press, 1984–88), 3 (1988), trans. Kathleen Blamey and David Pellauer, 154.

2. Cathy Caruth, "The Claims of Reference," in *Critical Encounters: Reference and Responsibility in Deconstructive Writing*, ed. Cathy Caruth and Deborah Esch (New Brunswick: Rutgers University Press, 1995), 92, 94.

3. Linda Hutcheon, *The Politics of Postmodernism* (New York: Routledge, 1989), 78.

4. Ian Haywood, *Faking It: Art and the Politics of Forgery* (New York: St. Martin's Press, 1987), 5.

5. Ian Haywood, *The Making of History: A Study of the Literary Forgeries of James Macpherson and Thomas Chatterton in Relation to Eighteenth-Century Ideas of History and Fiction* (Cranbury, N.J.: Associated University Presses, 1986), chap. 5. For a discussion of the social materiality of forgeries in the eighteenth century, see also Paul Baines, "'Our Annius': Antiquaries and Fraud in the Eighteenth Century," *British Journal for Eighteenth-Century Studies* 20 (1997): 33–52.

6.   . . . he
> Who casts to write a living line, must sweat,
> (Such as thine are) and strike the second heat
> Upon the Muses anvile: turne the same,
> (And himself with it) that he thinkes to frame;
> Or for the lawrell, he may gaine a scorne,
> For a good Poet's made, as well as borne.
>
> ("To the Memory of my Beloved, the Author,
> Mr. William Shakespeare," ll. 58–64)

Haywood lists the following meanings of "forgery" from the *OED:*

1. The action or craft of forging metal.
1b. A piece of forged work (rare).
2. Invention, excogitation; fictitious invention, fiction.
3. The making of a thing in fraudulent imitation of something; also, esp. the forging, counterfeiting, or falsifying of a document.
3c. Something forged, counterfeited, or fabricated; a spurious production. (*Faking It*, 6)

Haywood notes that "around the time of the Renaissance (the earliest quotation mustered is 1574) the concept [of forgery] was abstracted from the concrete world to apply to the mind's creative faculties . . . . Yet fiction and forgery are blood relatives . . . . A forgery is still a making: its condemnation is a matter of interpretation and law. Forgery is only a threat when there is the possibility of 'prejudicing another [person's] right,' as the falsifying of documents is supposed to do. In terms of art, this right can only be 'prejudiced' if art is regarded as individualised, original creation" (*Faking It*, 6).

7. Nick Groom with Charlie Blake, "Introduction," *Narratives of Forgery*, ed. Nick Groom, *Angelaki* 1, no. 2 (Winter 93/94): 6.

8. Ibid.; see also Nick Groom, "Forgery or Plagiarism? Unravelling Chatterton's Rowley" (ibid., 41–54) and Randall McGowen, "Forgery Discovered or the Perils of Circulation in Eighteenth-Century England" (ibid., 113–29).

9. For Chatterton's psychological search for and artistic invention of a beneficent, heroic father in his forgeries, see Donald S. Taylor, *Thomas Chatterton's Art: Experiments in Imagined History* (Princeton: Princeton University Press, 1978), chap. 2, and Louise J. Kaplan, *The Family Romance of the Imposter-Poet Thomas Chatterton* (New York: Atheneum, 1988), chap. 4. For Lacanian and Foucaultian readings of the same material, see Susan Stewart, *Crimes of Writing: Problems in the Containment of Representation* (Durham, N.C.: Duke University Press, 1994), chap. 5. Of the first "published" attempt to invent an ideal past for Bristol, Taylor remarks: "The 'Bridge Narrative' is a detailed set of stage directions for an elaborate, colorful civic pageant expressive of Chatterton's senses of a holy and heroic Bristol past and a community of feeling in religion, art, and civic life" (*Thomas Chatterton's Art,* 108). The connection between the two discourses, the psychological search for the father and the (re)invention of the historical past for Bristol, is eloquently suggested by Chatterton's story that his father had found the manuscript of the *Bridge Narrative* in a coffer in the Muniment Room of St. Mary Redcliffe church, while in fact (and quite characteristically) Chatterton had envisioned the piece himself in response to the events surrounding the opening of the new Bristol bridge in October 1768; see E. H. W. Meyerstein, *A Life of Thomas Chatterton* (New York: Scribners, 1930), 106, 110.

10. The drawings illustrated the various manuscripts, and are now in the British Library and the Bristol Public Library. For the manuscripts and the early editions of Chatterton's works, see *The Complete Works of Thomas Chatterton,* ed. Donald S. Taylor, in association with Benjamin B. Hoover, 2 vols. (Oxford: Clarendon Press, 1971), 1:xxv–xxxi. Taylor's edition reproduces many of the drawings.

11. See Benedict Anderson, *Imagined Communities: Reflections on the Origin and Spread of Nationalism* (London: Verso, 1983), chaps. 2 and 3. Anderson's basic argument is that "the convergence of capitalism and print technology on the fatal diversity of human language created the possibility of a new form of imagined community, which in its basic morphology set the stage for the modern nation" (49).

12. Nick Groom, review of *Thomas Chatterton: Early Sources and Responses,* 6 vols. (London: Routledge/Thoemmes Press, 1993), in *Narratives of Forgery,* 160.

13. Stewart, *Crimes of Writing,* 150.

14. For Chatterton's dealings with Horace Walpole, see also Meyerstein, *Life,* 253–84, and Taylor, *Thomas Chatterton's Art,* 66–71.

15. Walpole wrote: "Give me leave to ask you where Rowley's poems are to be found. I shall not be sorry to print them, or at least a specimen of them, if they have never been printed" (quoted by Taylor, *Thomas Chatterton's Art,* 68). As Taylor observes, Walpole's interest is initially piqued by the *Ryse* because "Walpole had been able to name no artists before the reign of King John . . . [and] he had had to be imprecise about the beginnings of glass staining and wall painting, and in the first two chapters [of *Anecdotes of Painting*] he had frequently returned to the idea that oil painting could have predated Van Eyck, even suggesting that Van Eyck might have learned the technique in England" (*Thomas Chatterton's Art,* 67). All of these doubts were "settled" by Chatterton to Walpole's satisfaction in his imagined history or prefifteenth-century art.

16. *Horace Walpole's Correspondence,* ed. W. S. Lewis, 48 vols. (New Haven: Yale University Press, 1937–83), 16 (1951): 127–28 (letter to William Bewley, 23 May 1778). This letter (122–34) gives Walpole's whole narrative of his dealings with Chatterton.

17. This, notwithstanding Walpole's own earlier *Castle of Otranto* which claims, in the preface to the first edition (1765), to be the work of an editor who translated a sixteenth-century Italian text (supposedly published in 1529), which itself supposedly existed in a manuscript written between 1095 and 1243 in "the pureest Italian"; see *The Castle of Otranto,* ed. W. S. Lewis (Oxford: Oxford University Press, 1982), 3. It is significant that Walpole chooses to veil his fictional purposes by forging a translation. In doing this, but in a lower register, he anticipates Chatterton, and posits a nonexistent past to revive and to translate in order to make his statement about politics, authority, and history; see also Lee Morrissey, "'To invent in art and folly': Postmodernism and Walpole's *Castle of Otranto,*" in *Bucknell Review* 41, no. 2: *Questioning History: The Postmodern Turn to the Eighteenth Century,* ed. Greg Clingham. Chatterton registered the irony of Walpole's position in his poem "To Horace Walpole": "didst thou ne'er indulge in such Deceit? / Who wrote *Otranto?*" (ll. 6–7). The poem also clearly indicates how closely bound up the Rowley forgeries were with Chatterton's sense of personal fame and immortality: "But I shall live and stand / By *Rowley's* side, when thou art dead and damn'd" (ll. 16–17).

18. Haywood, *The Making of History,* 151.

19. Caruth, "The Claims of Reference," in *Critical Encounters,* 94.

20. Groom and Blake, "Introduction," *Narratives of Forgery,* 6.

21. See particularly Linda Hutcheon, *The Poetics of Postmodernism: History, Theory, Fiction* (New York: Routledge, 1988), esp. chaps. 7 and 8, and *The Politics of Postmodernism,* esp. chap. 3; Donna Heiland, "Historical Subjects: Recent Fiction about the Eighteenth Century," *Eighteenth-Century Life* 21 (1997): 108–22; and Clingham, ed., *Questioning History* (*Bucknell Review* 41, no. 2).

22. Hutcheon, *Poetics of Postmodernism,* 118.

23. Peter Ackroyd, *Chatterton: A Novel* (1987; New York: Ballantine Books, 1989); hereafter *C,* cited in the text.

24. Ricoeur, *Time and Narrative,* 3:119.

25. Ibid., 120.

26. Hutcheon, *Politics of Postmodernism,* 94, 78. For Hutcheon's reading of Ackroyd's *Chatterton* as "a postmodern novel whose form and content denaturalize representation in both visual and verbal media," see *Politics,* 95–98.

27. See, e.g., Hutcheon, *Poetics of Postmodernism,* 106; and Hayden White, "The Historical Text as Literary Artefact" and "The Fictions of Factual Representation" in White, *Tropics of Discourse: Essays in Cultural Criticism* (Baltimore: Johns Hopkins University Press, 1978). Needless to say, I find the work of both Hutcheon and White to be invaluable in formulating my argument in this essay and in considering new developments in historiography.

28. Nancy Armstrong and Leonard Tennenhouse, "History, Poststructuralism, and the Question of Narrative," *Narrative* 1 (1993): 45–58, esp. 50. I am, however, sympathetic to Armstrong's and Tennenhouse's concern that "Poststructuralism inevitably reveals a formalist tendency to detach the object of analysis from the story of its production and reception" (50), and I try in this essay to maintain the sense of difficult and shifting relationships between the "object of analysis" and the "story of its production," especially difficult when the "object"—history—is itself the means by which it is known.

29. There is no mention of Samuel Joynson in Chatterton scholarship. The Rowley works were made public by George Catcott and William Barrett, both of whom suspected Chatterton of forgery. See Meyerstein, *Life,* chap. 10. Ackroyd's seemingly authentic depiction of the eighteenth-century Bristol publisher Joynson is one of several ingenious touches by which he is able to create a concrete sense of the forged yet quite real world that Chatterton himself invented through text.

30. This aspect of Ackroyd's irony asks to be compared to the skeptical intelligence of Milan Kundera's *The Book of Laughter and Forgetting* and *Laughable Loves;* see Felicity Rosslyn, "Czech Neo-Classicism," *The Cambridge Quarterly* 11 (1983): 424–29.

31. To an extraordinary degree, Chatterton's many biographers have contested the facts and the motives of his death. For a useful survey see Kaplan, *Thomas Chatterton,* chap. 9, and Meyerstein, *Life,* chap. 19. On the accidental death theory, see, e.g., Richard Holmes, "Thomas Chatterton: The Case Re-Opened," *Cornhill Magazine* 178 (1970): 244.

32. See Greg Clingham, "Introduction: The Question of History and Eighteenth-Century Studies," in *Questioning History (Bucknell Review* 41, no. 2).

33. Chatterton's Bristol collaborator, William Barrett, a surgeon when not pursuing his antiquarian researches, wrote as follows of Chatterton's death in his *History of Bristol* (1789): "He took a large dose of opium, some of which was picked out from between his teeth after death, and he was found the next morning a most horrid spectacle, with limbs and features distorted as after convulsions, a frightful and ghastly corpse" (quoted in Meyerstein, *Life,* 436). As Meyerstein remarks, Barrett knew that opium alone could not produce those symptoms, and he was instrumental in qualifying the coroner's less than scientific diagnosis, and suggesting that the death was accidental.

34. John Ruskin, *The Works of John Ruskin,* ed. E. T. Cook and Alexander Wedderburn, 39 vols. (London, 1903–12): 14:60 (quoted from Malcolm Warner, *The Victorians: British Painting, 1837–1901* (Washington: National Gallery of Art, 1997), 102. Wallis's picture was bought by Augustus Egg, who had it engraved by T. P. Barlow, and who wrote, "Others . . . will suppose that a picture portraying 'The Death of Chatterton' will be painful: nothing of the kind; —here the most refined and sensitive cannot be offended. The Artist has invested his subject with a charm, a fascination that binds you to it, and is beyond description. It is the essence of poetry and teaches a moral beyond the power and capabilities of language"; quoted in Diane Johnson, *The True History of the First Mrs. Meredith and Other Lesser Lives* (New York: Knopf, 1972), 92. For Wallis's painting in the context of romanticism, see Marcia Pointon, "Romanticism in English Art," in *Romantics,* ed. Stephen Prickett (New York: Holmes & Meier, 1981), 88–94.

35. John Ruskin, *The Lamp of Beauty: Writings on Art,* selected and ed. Joan Evans (1959; reprint, London: Phaidon, 1995), 53; hereafter *LB,* cited in the text.

36. Vincent Van Gogh's comment on color is applicable to the practice of the Pre-Raphaelites in general, including Wallis—"the colours on the palette [rather] than . . . the colours in nature"—to "make those very incorrectnesses, those deviations, remodelling changes of reality, so that they may become. yes, untruth if you like—but more true than the literal truth"; see *The Letters of Van Gogh,* ed. Mark Roskill (London: Fontana, 1979), 240, 236, and passim.

37. Consider Ruskin's thought about the power of some of the colors used by Wallis, as imagined by Ackroyd: "I think nature mixes yellow with almost every

one of her hues, never, or very rarely, using red without it, but frequently using yellow with scarcely any red; and I believe it will be in consequence found that her favourite opposition, that which generally characterizes and gives tone to her colour, is yellow and black, passing, as it retires, into white and blue" (*Lamp of Beauty*, 15–16).

38. Marcia Pointon writes of the "shocking image" the painting presents by implicitly associating the "suicide of a fraud and the death of Christ," and by exploiting "a long pictorial tradition of heroic death-bed scenes, which originated with the specifically Christian *Extreme Unction* of Poussin" ("Romanticism in English Art," 92).

39.   At the still point of the turning world. Neither flesh nor fleshless;
        Neither from nor towards; at the still point, there the dance is,
        But neither arrest nor movement. And do not call it fixity,
        Where past and future are gathered.

                                    (T. S. Eliot, "Burnt Norton," ll. 62–65)

Ackroyd is, of course, a biographer of Eliot.

40. For Ackroyd's fictional purposes it does not matter that the exact location of Chatterton's garret may not have been detected till 1857; see Malcolm Warner, *The Victorians*, 101.

41. Barbara Stafford writes of James Rosen's postmodern imitations of the paintings of Joshua Reynolds, *Homages to Reynolds:* "Their physical indeterminacy and optical minimalism simultaneously promise a glimpse into the eighteenth century while withholding the possibility of ever recuperating that era in its rich coloration and volumetric palpability"; see Stafford, *Good Looking: Essays on the Virtue of Images* (Cambridge: MIT Press, 1996), 63.

42. See Hutcheon, *Politics of Postmodernism:* "Wallis' painting of Meredith *creates* the death of Chatterton for posterity through its representation" (97).

43. W. Holman Hunt, *Pre-Raphaelitism and the Pre-Raphaelite Brotherhood*, 2 vols. (London, 1905), 2:417, quoted in Pointon, "Romanticism in English Art," 94.

44. See, e.g., Ricoeur, *Time and Narrative*, 3:152–53, and White, *Tropics of Discourse*, 106.

45. John Serle argues that there is "no textual property, syntactical, or semantic [or, consequently, narratological] that will identify a text as a work of fiction," because the fictional narrative is simply a simulation of factual narrative; see Serle, *Expression and Meaning* (Cambridge: Cambridge University Press, 1979), 65. See also Gerard Genette's discussion of this issue in *Fiction and Diction*, trans. Catherine Porter (Ithaca: Cornell University Press, 1991), chap. 3, "Fictional Narrative, Factual Narrative." For the relation between forgery and history in James Macpherson's *Ossian*, see *The Poems of Ossian and Related Works*, ed. Howard Gaskill, with an introduction by Fiona Stafford (Edinburgh: Edinburgh University Press, 1996), v–xviii.

46. Hayden White, *The Content of the Form: Narrative Discourse and Historical Representation* (Baltimore: Johns Hopkins University Press, 1987), 49. I have identified translation as the particular form of postmodern historical narrative in Jeanette Winterson's *Sexing the Cherry*, in "Winterson's Fiction and Enlightenment Historiography," in *Questioning History* (*Bucknell Review* 41, no. 2). See also Greg Clingham, "Translating Difference: The Example of Dryden's *Last Parting of Hector and Andromache*," in *Studies in the Literary Imagination*, Special Edition:

"Translation, Imitation and the Eighteenth-Century Imagination (1660–1800): Theory, Practice and Pedagogy," ed. Tanya Caldwell (forthcoming).

47. Walter Benjamin, "Theses on the Philosophy of History," in *Illuminations*, ed. Hannah Arendt, trans. Harry Zohn (New York: Schocken Books, 1969), 261, 263; Benedict Anderson, *Imagined Communities*, chap. 2. For a provocative discussion of the way in which temporalities and texts are shaped by clocks, calendars, and print in the long eighteenth century, see Stuart Sherman, *Telling Time: Clocks, Diaries, and English Diurnal Form, 1660–1785* (Chicago: University of Chicago Press, 1996), esp. chap. 1.

48. Homi K. Bhabha, *The Location of Culture* (London: Routledge, 1994). In what follows I am also indebted to an unpublished article, "Nation-Text: Griselda Then and Now," by my colleague Kathleen Davis.

49. Homi K. Bhabha, "How Newness Enters the World," in *The Location of Culture*, 228.

50. Ibid., 224. Bhabha refers to Walter Benjamin, "The Task of the Translator," in *Illuminations*, 75.

51. Anderson, *Imagined Communities*, 30.

52. Frank Kermode, *The Sense of an Ending: Studies in the Theory of Fiction* (1966; reprint, London: Oxford University Press, 1968), 46.

53. Sherman, *Telling Time*, 24. Sherman points out that Kermode's theory of narrative does not maintain the antithesis, taking its origin from the New Testament, between *chronos* (passing time) and *kairos* (a point in time filled with significance, charged with a meaning derived from its relation to the end) that it seems to imply, because "according to the Greek, *chronos (Tick, Tick, Tick)* is as susceptible of fullness *(pleroma)* as is *kairos (tick-tock)*" (*Telling Time*, 24).

54. Caruth, "The Claims of Reference," in *Critical Encounters*, 103. See Paul de Man, "The Resistance to Theory," in *The Resistance to Theory* (Minneapolis: University of Minnesota Press, 1986).

"A by-stander often sees more of the game than those that play": Ann Yearsley Reads *The Castle of Otranto*

Madeleine Kahn
Mills College

WHEN Horace Walpole heard that the bluestocking Hannah More had given his novella *The Castle of Otranto* to her protégé, Ann Yearsley, to read, he chastised his friend for thinking an uneducated milkwoman such as Yearsley would be able to read his Gothic tale in the spirit in which he wrote it:

> What! if I should . . . take the liberty of reproving you for putting into this poor woman's hands such a frantic thing as the *Castle of Otranto*? It was fit for nothing but the age in which it was written, an age [which did not care] whether its amusements were conformable to truth and the models of good sense; . . . but you will have made a hurly-burly in this poor woman's head which it cannot develop and digest. . . . her imagination is already too gloomy, and should be enlivened.[1]

Walpole clearly expects Yearsley to be an impressionable and therefore unsophisticated reader. He imagines that she will take the Gothic fancies of *Otranto* too literally and so be terrified and confused by them. In at least one respect he turned out to be correct: as Yearsley's poem on the topic, "TO THE HONOURABLE H——E W——E, on READING THE CASTLE OF OTRANTO. December, 1784,"[2] tells us, she was quite an impressionable reader and, at least for the purposes of her poem, she professed to be terrified by some of the supernatural events in the novella:

> Thy jawless skeleton of JOPPA's wood
> Stares in my face, and frights my mental eye;
>
> (ll. 69–70)

I shudder, see the taper sinks in night,
He rises, and his fleshless form reveals.

(ll. 75–76)

Here Yearsley's speaker shares the terror of one of Walpole's characters; the world of *Otranto* is real to her. These lines seem to offer support for Walpole's idea that Yearsley is too unsophisticated and too gloomy by nature to be an appropriate reader for *Otranto*. The editor of Walpole's letters, W. S. Lewis, quotes them as proof that Walpole was correct, but I believe Lewis has mistaken one small part of the poem for the burden of the whole. Yearsley's response to *Otranto* is not limited to this fearful credulity, nor is her relationship to Walpole simply that of an unlettered reader to a skilled author. But in one way Lewis is quite right to cite these lines as typical, for they are a good example of the way Yearsley's poem renders her reading experience so immediate. She writes in the present tense; she relives the terror and misery of each of the characters; she addresses Walpole as if he were in the midst of writing his tale at that very moment and as if she could influence the outcome if she argues passionately enough. In all of these ways she is as susceptible a reader as Walpole fears.

Furthermore, Yearsley agreed with Walpole that his story was so terrifying that some readers should be protected from its effects—but the reader she in turn warned away was Walpole's fellow-member of the literary elite, Hannah More (referred to here as in other poems as Stella):

> STELLA! if WALPOLE's spectres thus can scare,
>   Then near that great Magician's walls ne'er tread,
> He'll surely conjure many a spirit there,
>   Till, fear-struck, thou art number'd with the dead.
>
> Oh! with this noble Sorcerer ne'er converse,
>   Fly, STELLA, quickly from the magic storm;

(ll. 81–86)

Clearly while she agrees that *Otranto* is not suitable for some readers, Yearsley does not share Walpole's belief that the better-educated and higher-class reader will prove less susceptible to the terrors of his story than she herself. Rather she assumes that she is hardy enough to converse "with this noble Sorcerer" Walpole, but that Stella, her superior in class, education, and literary background, is not. In fact, her entire poem stands on its head Walpole's assumption that those who are impressionable cannot also be sophisticated readers and critics. Her poem demonstrates that far from making her an unfit reader, being impressionable makes her instead the most passionately involved and generous reader of the *Castle of Otranto* that Walpole could have hoped for.

Yearsley is so willingly receptive to Walpole's text that she responds wholeheartedly even to those aspects of the story that he deemed inconsequential. She takes note of what goes on around the main action, in the lives of the women and the servants on the edges of the convoluted plot. For example, she uses Walpole's character Bianca, a servant in the castle, as the first-person speaker of her poem. As Bianca she addresses many of Walpole's other characters directly in her poem, identifying with them, and responding as if the tale depicted real people in intolerable situations. Her empathy for these characters prompts her to make their relationships and their internal struggles more important in her poem than the working out of the prophecy about who shall inherit the castle of Otranto. This shift in focus toward the characters and away from the plot leads her to criticize Walpole for the short shrift he gives those characters (especially the women) even as she praises him for his skill in creating the fictional world that has so captivated her. Speaking in the first person through Bianca, Yearsley addresses Walpole directly and, using both sticks and carrots, tries to cajole him into sharing her experience of the story he has written.

Yearsley's Bianca begins aggressively, venting her bitterness at the artificial limits Walpole has placed on her intelligence and her voice. In Walpole's tale Bianca seems to be merely a voluble and flighty servant in the castle, and Walpole is on record in his two prefaces as dismissing her as unimportant. In the first preface he offers this interpretation of the servants' roles in the story:

> Some persons may perhaps think the character of the domestics too little serious for the general cast of the story; but . . . [t]hey discover many passages essential to the story, which could not well be brought to light but by their *naivete* and simplicity; in particular, the womanish terror and foibles of Bianca, in the last chapter, conduce essentially towards advancing the catastrophe.[3]

According to Walpole the servants are not so much characters as they are devices to advance the plot. He goes further in his second preface to expand on this argument that the "domestics," as he calls them, function as a dramatic device (rather than as characters) to heighten the seriousness and the portentousness of the rest of the story. Here he appeals to both the "rule [of] nature" and to that "higher authority . . . [t]hat great master of nature, Shakespeare" for his assertion that:

> However grave, important, or even melancholy, the sensations of princes and heroes may be, they do not stamp the same affections on their domestics: at least the latter do not, or should not be made to express their passions in the same dignified tone. In my humble opinion, the contrast between the sublime of the one and the *naivete* of the other, sets the pathetic of the former in a stronger light. (*CO*, 8)

This argument continues for another four pages, with ample quotations from both Shakespeare and Voltaire, and I read it as Walpole's indirect acknowledgment that the servants end up occupying a large part of his tale and that he needs in some way to account for their prominence. His method is to say that although they take up space, they are not important in their own right.

Yearsley's Bianca takes offense at this characterization of her as a creature of "womanish terror and foibles" who is significant only for the ways in which she furthers events or promotes the development of other characters. By choosing Bianca for her poetic persona Yearsley shows us that even in Walpole's version Bianca is the figure in the story who grasps the import of both the natural and the supernatural events and who sees the true nature of her fellow characters. In her poem Yearsley builds on Walpole's characterization to develop Bianca further into the figure who can address both praise and criticism to Walpole on behalf of his other characters. Bit by bit Yearsley's Bianca grows into a character who can assert that being a serving maid makes her a shrewd and necessary commentator on Walpole's story, not a flighty character whose "womanish foibles" obstruct the story's development. In Yearsley's poem Bianca achieves significance as an independent character because Yearsley makes hers the voice of the internal ideal reader of *The Castle of Otranto*. Thus Yearsley has Bianca demonstrate for the world within Walpole's fiction what her poem demonstrates for the world of the reader: just as Yearsley's passionate susceptibility to Walpole's authorial powers makes her an exceptional reader rather than an unfit one, so Bianca's supposed marginality as a servant turns out to be the asset that allows her a broader perspective on the work in which she appears.

As the poem opens, however, Yearsley's Bianca has not yet broken out of the role Walpole has given her. Instead she is chafing at that role from within its confines and bitterly decrying her inability to speak because of the limitations Walpole has placed on her:

> To praise thee, WALPOLE, asks a pen divine,
>   And common sense to me is hardly given,
> BIANCA's Pen now owns the daring line,
>   And who expects *her* muse should drop from Heaven.
>
> (ll. 1–4)

At first Yearsley's Bianca can only repeat with bitter emphasis what Walpole would say of her:

> Supreme in prate shall woman ever sit,
>   While Wisdom smiles to hear the senseless squall;
> Nature, who gave me tongue, deny'd me wit,
>   Folly I worship, and she claims me all.
>
> (ll. 13–16)

And yet even in these opening lines we can see that although Yearsley has chosen one of Walpole's characters for her persona and so is speaking from inside the world of *Otranto,* she also uses Bianca to voice her own perspective so that Yearsley's Bianca is also the milkwoman poet addressing one of the most exalted aesthetes of the day. The poem is never a dramatic monologue; both the speaker and the implied audience shift back and forth from the world inside the poem to the world of the poet.

In these two stanzas Yearsley beats Walpole over the head with his portrait of Bianca. She has loosed his own character upon him, now giving Bianca's pen ownership of the "daring line" and forcing Walpole to attend to "The empty tattle, true to female rules, / In which thy happier talents ne'er appear" (ll. 9–10). And, she warns, there will be no praise of Walpole here, because that would take a "pen divine" and we all know Bianca's muse is not going to "drop from Heaven." This aggressive beginning essentially dares Walpole to dismiss what Yearsley has to say because she has chosen to write in Bianca's voice.

Such a ferocious beginning would seem to promise a poem promoting literary anarchy, in which the fictional character chastises her creator and rewrites her story as she wants it to be told. But almost immediately Yearsley's poem turns away from such anarchy toward an awed, almost docile appreciation of Walpole's powers. The several stanzas which directly follow Bianca's opening outburst are more like the lines cited by W. S. Lewis; they narrate

Bianca's empathetic involvement with the other characters and with the terrors they face.

This section begins with the lines, "The drowsy eye, half-closing to the lid, / Stares on OTRANTO's walls; grim terrors rise" (ll. 17–18). Here Yearsley's Bianca enters into a near dream state, in which she appears to be hypnotized by the specters and spectacles of Walpole's world of Otranto. "Funereal plumes now wave; ALPHONSO's ghost / Frowns o'er my shoulder;" (ll. 21–22). In this state she directly addresses her fellow characters and their mutual creator, Walpole. To Manfred she says, "I feel thy agonies in WALPOLE's line," (l. 30) and then she turns to Walpole himself, hailing his "magic pen" (l. 33) and then demanding, "Where's MANFRED's refuge? WALPOLE, tell me where?" (l. 37).

This challenge to the author marks another shift in the tone of Yearsley's poem from awe-struck admiration for Walpole to eager advocacy for his characters. After her address to Manfred, Yearsley's Bianca turns to the women: Matilda, Hippolita, and Isabella. As she addresses them, she becomes increasingly exercised at the positions in which Walpole and his character Manfred have the women confined. She moves from a more descriptive exclamation:

> MATILDA! ah, how soft thy yielding mind,
> When hard obedience cleaves thy timid heart!
>
> (ll. 41–42)

to a more critical one:

> HYPOLITA! fond, passive to excess,
> Her low submission suits not souls like mine;
> BIANCA might have lov'd her MANFRED less.[4]
>
> (ll. 49–51)

Over the course of these six stanzas which begin with her apostrophe to Matilda, Yearsley's Bianca moves from submissive awe at Walpole's powers to empathy with his downtrodden women characters, then to a declaration of her own "omnipotence," and finally to straightforward bargaining with the formerly awe-inspiring Walpole. This part of the poem is crucial to the development of Yearsley's Bianca and of her critique of Walpole's art.

Right after she asserts that she "might have lov'd her MANFRED less," Yearsley's Bianca emerges from the specifics of Walpole's story and characters to make a general pronouncement about the way women submit to men:

> Implicit Faith, all hail! Imperial man
>   Exacts submission; reason we resign;
> Against our senses we adopt the plan
>   Which Reverence, Fear, and Folly think divine.

(ll. 53–56)

In these lines Yearsley's Bianca speaks from a perspective beyond the limits of what Walpole has allowed her. She has a greater scope than she does earlier in this same poem where she either chafes at her restrictions without being able to analyze them ("Supreme in prate shall woman ever sit," l. 13), or is wholly captivated by Walpole's spell ("grim terrors rise, / The horrid helmet strikes my soul unbid," ll. 18–19). As Bianca's voice develops we can also hear Ann Yearsley speaking from outside Walpole's story, expressing solidarity with the practically voiceless women in the text who must conceal what they know. Yearsley emerges even more directly in the next two stanzas in which she sets the terms for a deal with Walpole: Your character Bianca will keep silent about what she knows about "you MANFREDS," thereby leaving your tale intact, but in exchange you must "Ope the trap-door where all thy powers reside," and tell me your secrets, author to author:

> But be it so, BIANCA ne'er shall prate,
>   Nor ISABELLA's equal powers reveal;
> You MANFREDS boast your power, and prize your state;
>   We ladies our omnipotence conceal.
>
> But, Oh! then strange-inventing WALPOLE guide,
>   Ah! guide me thro' thy subterranean isles,
> Ope the trap-door where all thy powers reside,
>   And mimic Fancy real woe beguiles.

(ll. 57–64)

In these stanzas Yearsley seems to abandon temporarily the persona of Bianca to speak to Walpole as a fellow author. For the plea to "ope the trap-door where all thy powers reside" is that of an author, not a character in *The Castle of Otranto*. It becomes clear that in the previous stanza it is Yearsley who will keep Bianca from "prating" and revealing "ISABELLA's equal powers," and who will her own "omnipotence conceal." In these stanzas Yearsley is making explicit the bargain she has fulfilled in this poem: I'll be an obedient and credulous participant in your fantasy (both the supernatural goings on at Otranto and the portraits of Manfred and others as "Imperial man") right down to giving up my voice for the voice of one of your own characters. But in exchange I want the secret of your literary power.

Certainly the poem's speaker is far more powerful and assertive in these lines than she was earlier in the poem when she was helpless before Walpole's literary power, either as his limited creation who can merely prattle, or as his spellbound reader who dies when his characters die (l. 20). However, Yearsley does not forfeit her susceptibility in order to claim this new forcefulness. For example, she wants access to Walpole's powers, but she has no desire to destroy or belittle them; she wants to be able to use them. For as Walpole saw, Yearsley's imagination was gloomy. And, as he does not mention, her life was hard.[5] She feels "real woe," and she is in need of "mimic Fancy" to beguile that woe away. Her poem returns to the power of that "mimic Fancy" right after this plea, narrating once again the susceptible reader's experience of *The Castle of Otranto*. Indeed, the awe-struck lines cited by Lewis appear just two stanzas after Yearsley/Bianca's attempt at blackmail. These heartfelt passages of pure readerly surrender further demonstrate that for all its aggression and criticism, Yearsley's poem is foremost an appreciation of Walpole's tale.

With this return to the effect *Otranto* has had on her, the poem's speaker also begins to consider other readers. She first turns to her primary interlocutor, the woman with whom she was engaged in an ongoing literary and personal conversation throughout the period in which she was writing the *Poems on Several Occasions,* Hannah More.[6] She warns "Stella" away from close conversation with Walpole's tale with the lines I've already quoted (ending with "Fly, STELLA, quickly from the magic storm" (l. 86). She then elaborates on the risks that reading Walpole entails:

> Trust not his art, for should he stop thy breath,
>   And good ALPHONSO's ghost unbidden rise;
> He'd vanish, leave thee in the jaws of death,
>   And quite forget to close thy aching eyes.
>
> (ll. 89–92)

Under the guise of warning Stella, Yearsley/Bianca here asserts that Walpole is raising specters he cannot control and creating images whose full effect on his readers he cannot possibly know. This suggestion is in keeping with the rest of Yearsley's reading of Walpole's tale: she asserts that in Bianca (and to some extent the other women) Walpole has created a character whose full powers and worth he ignores. She goes further to suggest that in the tale as a whole, which he affected to dismiss as "a frantic thing," he has inserted challenges to the gender and class hierarchies that the world of *Otranto* seems so determinedly to support.

Like so much else in Yearsley's poem, these perceptions about the limits of Walpole's art and of his control over his characters contain a mixture of criticism and admiration. He has the power to "stop thy breath," the speaker says, but he'll "forget" to offer you comfort, "to close thy aching eyes." Similarly, he has the instinct to create the character of Bianca, but not the insight to use her fully in his tale.

Yearsley aims in her poem to add what she feels is missing from Walpole's tale. In this too she is following Walpole's lead, and even offering homage to him. For, although Yearsley broadens the scope of Walpole's Bianca as she enriches the character's voice in her poem, she is building on the character that Walpole created. Yearsley never strays too far from Walpole's Bianca. In fact, the argument that she makes for Bianca as well as for herself—that outsider status is a source of insight, not blindness—comes directly from something that Walpole's Bianca says in *The Castle of Otranto:* "A by-stander often sees more of the game than those that play" (*CO*, 43). When she says this, Walpole's Bianca is speculating to her mistress, Matilda, about an attachment between Matilda's friend, Isabella, and the mysteriously noble peasant, Theodore. Her assertion that "he tells you he is in love, or unhappy, it is the same thing" (43) is just one of the many instances in which Walpole's Bianca sees clearly what to other characters is shrouded in mist. At times her greater detachment even seems like a kind of readerly literary sophistication. In the matter of Theodore, for example, only Bianca seems to know the conventions of literary romance.

Walpole's own Bianca is clearly aware that her outsider status as a servant is anything but the handicap that it might seem to be. Instead it allows her greater mobility and more opportunity to speak than the other women characters. Especially in the last chapter, Bianca displays how she uses her "womanish terrors" to manipulate her master, Manfred, and her seemingly senseless prattle to speak the truth. In this chapter, she tortures Manfred with insinuations about Isabella's attachment to Theodore, and she thwarts his efforts to hide his stratagems from Isabella's father, Frederick. For example, when Manfred, plotting to marry Isabella himself, tries bribing Bianca to find out "how long . . .

Isabella [has] been acquainted with Theodore," she effectively heightens his anxiety while telling him nothing:

> Nay, there is nothing can escape your highness . . . —not that I know anything of the matter. Theodore, to be sure, is a proper young man, and, as my lady Matilda says, the very image of good Alfonso: Has not your highness remarked it? Yes, yes—No—thou torturest me, said Manfred: Where did they meet? when?—Who, my lady Matilda? said Bianca. (*CO*, 97)

It is perhaps a mark of Walpole's backhanded acknowledgment of Bianca's power that he particularly cites this last chapter as evidence of Bianca's frivolity, and of her limited function as a device for advancing the plot, or as he put it, "the catastrophe" (*CO*, 4).

Walpole's instances of Bianca's foolishness paradoxically lead us—and presumably led Yearsley—to recognize how crucial she is to the story. The space he devotes in his prefaces to trying to confine Bianca to her role as a silly servant shows clearly that he knew that the character he had created didn't quite fit into the role he had assigned her. In her poem, Ann Yearsley pursues this belated insight of his and expands Bianca's role to fit the character Walpole had created. Instead of devaluing Bianca's insights by insisting that she is a mere prop to establish the greater nobility of the other characters as Walpole does in his prefaces, Yearsley lets her continue to speak as she does in Walpole's tale. As a result, Yearsley's poem, for all of its criticism of Walpole, offers us a generous reading of Bianca's character and of Walpole's novella as a whole. By setting up a dialogue between her poem and Walpole's novella, she gives more texture to the novella, which has been made richer by her attention to Bianca's character. In following his direction then, Yearsley continues to pay tribute to Walpole, even as she shows him how limiting his treatment of Bianca is.

Toward the end of the poem, when the speaker has clearly moved further outside the confines of Walpole's fictional world into the real world where Yearsley is both an admiring reader and an author in her own right, she professes to fear retaliation from Walpole and his dark art. Immediately after she warns Stella/More to "Trust not his art," Yearsley's Bianca asks:

> But is BIANCA safe in this slow vale?
>   For should his Goblins stretch their dusky wing,
> Would they not bruise me for the saucy tale,
>   Would they not pinch me for the truths I sing?

> Yet whisper not I've call'd him names, I fear
>   His ARIEL would my hapless sprite torment,
> He'd cramp my bones, and all my sinews tear,
>   Should STELLA blab the secret I'd prevent.
>
> (ll. 93–100)

"Stella" might "blab the secret" to Walpole because he is a friend of hers. In fact, More had enlisted him in her campaign to publish Yearsley's poems and had sent him several of the early ones for his commentary.[7] And, of course, Yearsley is being coy here: she needs Stella to blab; she needs Walpole as a reader. Her poem is addressed to him, and he is the reader she most needs to convince of the validity of her version of Bianca's character and of the value of the laboring woman's perspective on events in *The Castle of Otranto*. Even her reference to Shakespeare's Ariel is an appeal to collaboration, echoing as it does Walpole's claim to be following Shakespeare in his comic treatment of the servants in his tale.

In these stanzas purporting to fear retribution, but more subtly enticing a reaction from Walpole, Yearsley is using the doubleness of her poetic persona to particular advantage. She plays on the contrast between her image as a lowly servant who has no protection against Walpole's Ariel who could "cramp my bones, and all my sinews tear," and her clear confidence in her voice as Walpole's fellow author. In these stanzas both the saucy yet powerless Bianca of the first part of the poem and the more aggressive Yearsley/Bianca of the quid pro quo offer in the middle of the poem appear again. Here Yearsley uses them together, carrot and stick, to flatter and correct Walpole into joining with her in a conversation about his work.

Building on Walpole's own Bianca, who uses her status as a mere by-stander to see the game more clearly than "those that play," Yearsley uses her awe-struck and impressionable reading to reveal to Walpole, as well as to us, the full richness of Bianca's power as a character. In her poem she suggests that Bianca—not coincidentally like Yearsley herself—is not entirely defined by her class status. Being a servant in the castle, then, does not make her a mere by-stander; it makes her a crucial by-stander—as important to the game as "those that play." Thus Bianca's presence in Walpole's story authorizes the reading Yearsley proposes in her poem. Using his own character, his own language, and his own observation about outsider status, Yearsley proposes to Walpole that there are hidden riches in his Gothic tale. That is, she proposes that it is also true of the relationship between reader and author that "a by-stander often sees more of the game than those that play."

Yearsley's attempt to claim Walpole as a kind of before-the-fact collaborator in her version of the tale of *The Castle of Otranto* is both "daring," as she first asserts when she gives "BIANCA's Pen" ownership of "the daring line," and hopeful—she's paying homage to his creation. By seizing the outsider's perspective that Walpole has given to Bianca and providing more scope for her insights (such as her criticism of "Imperial man" and of Walpole as an author), Yearsley rescues the class and gender dynamics of *The Castle of Otranto* from the subterranean passages where Walpole had buried them. In so doing, she lends the tale depth and rescues the women characters and their relationships from the burden of the plot which threatens to bury them. I use the word "subterranean" advisedly of course, for the subterranean is crucial to both the physical and metaphorical landscapes of the Gothic. Specifically, in *Otranto* a trap door and a subterranean passage provide the way out of the castle for the beautiful Isabella when Manfred threatens her with a quasi-incestuous marriage. Only her knowledge of that subterranean passage frees the young woman from Manfred's plots and gives her the chance to express her own perspectives and desires. Similarly, when Yearsley's Bianca explicitly situates Walpole's literary power in his "subterranean isles" (l. 62) and asks him to "ope the trap-door where all thy powers reside" (l. 63), she is pleading for a way out of the realm in which she can only sit "supreme in prate" (l. 13) toward one in which she can "sing . . . the truths" (l. 96) she sees.

The experience of rereading *The Castle of Otranto* after reading Yearsley's poem is one of noticing how central much of what Walpole has pushed to the margins turns out to be. Walpole's own description of the tale as a "frantic thing" is correct if you try to read for the plot, which is both confusing and oddly skeletal. It concerns a stolen kingdom, a prophecy, a search for a male heir, and giant body parts which appear abruptly to derail the plans of Manfred, the usurper. The narrative of this part of the tale is not coherent enough to keep our attention; instead we wander off into the tangle of protean relationships among family members in the castle. These relationships are what Yearsley's poem first prompts the rereader to notice. When we begin to take the characters seriously, as she does, we see that most of the story is concerned with the characters' unexpected links to each other and the passions the revelations about those links release. The second insight Yearsley's poem offers the reader is that the male princes

and nobles make almost no sense as motivated characters: Conrad
is a cipher; Manfred is an appalling tyrant about whom the narrator nevertheless says, "Manfred was not one of those savage tyrants
who wanton in cruelty unprovoked" (CO, 30); and Frederick unre-
liably loses track of and then regains his desire to retrieve Isabella
from Manfred's clutches. The third thing we notice is that the
women and servants are far more richly drawn and are more
consistent as characters than the men. Their motivations and actions make sense; they respond more credibly to events and to
each other. These women and servants—and especially the
women servants—precisely because they are less fantastic than the
men—are the characters who give the reader a window into the
tale. As we reread we see that the women emerge as the focal
point of the tale. Even the plot finally works out to their advantage: Isabella marries Theodore; Hippolita retreats happily to a
convent; even Matilda, who is sacrificed to her father's murderous
rage is at least instrumental in his conversion (a fate which has
been presaged by her otherworldliness). We are not told specifically what happens to Bianca, but we can bet that she lands on
her feet as the personal maid to the new queen. She keeps a
careful eye on her own status from the beginning when she tries
to persuade Matilda that marriage would not be so bad. "I would
have you a great lady" (CO, 38) she says, knowing that she would
then "have the honour of being your highness's maid of honour"
(CO, 41).

By giving greater scope to Bianca's voice, then, Yearsley is making good on the hidden promises of Walpole's tale. By directing
our attention away from the men contesting over the kingdom of
Otranto, she restores coherence to our reading experience. Walpole had sacrificed this coherence by continually bringing the
men and their plots back to the foreground of his story. While
proposing that we (and Walpole) adopt her reading experience
as her own, however, Yearsley is careful never to suggest that she
wants to supplant Walpole as the author of The Castle of Otranto.
On the contrary, she returns again and again to the source of
her Bianca persona and her reading experience in Walpole's text.
Reminding us how rooted her poem is in Walpole's creation is
one of the purposes of the long passages of participatory reading,
such as this stanza in which Yearsley's Bianca empathizes with
Matilda, torn between duty and her love for Theodore:

> Ah, rigid duties, which two souls divide!
> Whose iron talons rend the panting breast!

> Pluck the dear image from the widow'd side,
> Where Love had lull'd its every care to rest.
>
> (ll. 45–48)

Even when she is most bitter, Yearsley's Bianca pays homage to Walpole's literary power. And even at the end of the poem, when Yearsley's Bianca has gained a more authoritative voice, she insists on Walpole's greater literary power. Each of her most daring moments, such as her offer of silence in exchange for guidance, and her daring Walpole to "bruise me for the saucy tale, / . . . pinch me for the truths I sing" (ll. 95–96) contains an acknowledgment of her susceptibility to Walpole's tale. She resists Walpole's either/or formulation: she is neither a susceptible nor a daring critic; she's both. The poem's ending acknowledges her susceptibility once more, and then goes a step further:

> But hush, ye winds, ye crickets chirp no more,
> I'll shrink to bed, nor these sad omens hear,
> An hideous rustling shakes the lattic'd door,
> His spirits hover in the sightless air.
>
> (ll. 101–04)

Just a few lines after she daringly and coyly warns Stella not to "blab the secret I'd prevent" (l. 100), Yearsley's Bianca succumbs once more to the terrifying images that Walpole has created. She "shrink[s] to bed" knowing that "his spirits" nevertheless "hover in the sightless air." The saucy and self-confident speaker who has earlier tried to cajole Walpole into seeing his own work through her eyes here longs to see nothing at all. She cannot free her mind of the spirits that Walpole has conjured there, so she pleads with a greater power, that of sleep, to "shut each entrance of my mind" and release her from Walpole's spell:

> Now, MORPHEUS, shut each entrance of my mind,
> Sink, sink, OTRANTO, in this vacant hour;
> To thee, Oh, balmy GOD! I'm all resign'd,
> To thee e'en WALPOLE's wand resigns its power.
>
> (ll. 105–08)

It takes a god, not a mere milkmaid poet to make "WALPOLE's wand resign its power." So Yearsley's poem concludes with great—if somewhat sad—admiration of Walpole. It also concludes with a retreat into silence, as if she is not quite sure she can sustain the voice she has created without Walpole's help.

Yearsley does not ask in this poem for Walpole to admire her as a fellow author. Rather she pleads for him to acknowledge her as a great reader of his work. She wants furthermore to show him that she is a great reader because of, rather than in spite of, the working-class and female perspective she brings to his work. These are some of her reasons for using Walpole's own character for the speaker of her poem; she wants to show him that her reading is as much a collaboration as a correction: she is following his lead.

In following that lead, and in expanding Bianca's character into what seems to be her more natural role, Yearsley is also participating in what was to become the great preoccupation of the Gothic novel in the eighteenth century: testing the limits of women's roles and exploring the indirect ways women might collaborate with—rather than simply be victimized by—the subterranean passions and powers beneath the roles that propriety allowed them. In the case of this milkmaid poet's daring to offer a corrective reading to Walpole's aesthetic experiment, this means most specifically suggesting that Walpole needs Yearsley as a sympathetic, collaborative reader to show him the riches in his own text. Still following his lead, Yearsley suggests to Walpole that this "bystander" has perhaps seen more in his novel than "those that play," that is, than he who first wrote it.

Notes

I presented a very early version of this paper at the conference "Rethinking Women's Poetry 1730–1930" in London, 21 July 1995. I am grateful for the feedback I got at that conference and for the travel grant from the American Council of Learned Societies, which enabled me to attend. I am also indebted to two of my best and most constant readers for their comments: Timothy Bishop and Cynthia Scheinberg. Thanks to Nancy Logan for the House of Work.

1. Horace Walpole to Hannah More, Saturday, 13 November 1784, in *Horace Walpole's Correspondence*, ed. W. S. Lewis, 48 vols. (New Haven: Yale University Press, 1938–83), 31 (1961): 221, n.12.

2. Ann Yearsley, *Poems on Several Occasions* (London: Cadell, 1785), 87–96. Citations will be by line number in the text. In these quotations from Yearsley's poem I have modernized the eighteenth-century long "s" but have otherwise kept the spelling and punctuation intact. The full 1785 text of the poem is given in an appendix to this essay.

3. Horace Walpole, "Preface to the First Edition," *The Castle of Otranto*, ed. W. S. Lewis (New York: Oxford University Press, 1982), 4; hereafter *CO*, cited in the text.

4. Yearsley changes Walpole's spelling "Hippolita" to "Hypolita."

5. At one point Yearsley, her husband, her children, and her mother were homeless and starving. Her mother died from the prolonged period of starvation, shortly after they were rescued. For biographical information on Ann Yearsley, see Hannah More, "A

Prefatory Letter to Mrs. Montagu. By a Friend," *Poems on Several Occasions;* J. M. S. Tompkins, *The Polite Marriage* (Cambridge: Cambridge University Press, 1938); Mary Waldron, "Ann Yearsley and the Clifton Records," *The Age of Johnson* 3 (1990): 301–29; and Linda Zionkowski, "Strategies of Containment: Stephen Duck, Ann Yearsley, and the Problem of Polite Culture," *Eighteenth-Century Life* 13, no. 3 (1989): 91–108.

6. For a detailed treatment of Yearsley's relationship to More as a collaborative one, see my article, "Hannah More and Ann Yearsley: A Collaboration across the Class Divide," *Studies in Eighteenth-Century Culture* 25 (1996): 203–23.

7. "I am surprised . . . at the dignity of her thoughts and the chastity of her style. Her ear, as you remark, is perfect . . . this good thing has real talents." Horace Walpole to Hannah More, 13 November 1784, *Correspondence,* 31: 219–20.

Appendix
Ann Yearsley
"To The
Honourable H___E W___E,
On Reading
THE CASTLE OF OTRANTO
December, 1784"

To praise thee, WALPOLE, asks a pen divine,
    And common sense to me is hardly given,
BIANCA's Pen now owns the daring line,
    And who expects *her* muse should drop from Heaven.

My fluttering tongue, light, ever veering round,
    On Wisdom's narrow point has never fix'd;
I dearly love to hear the ceaseless sound,
    Where Noise and Nonesense are completely mix'd.

The empty tattle, true to female rules,
    In which thy happier talents ne'er appear,
Is mine, nor mine alone, for mimic fools,
    Who boast *thy* sex, BIANCA's foibles wear.

Supreme in prate shall woman ever sit,
    While Wisdom smiles to hear the senseless squall;
Nature, who gave me tongue, deny'd me wit,
    Folly I worship, and she claims me all.

The drowsy eye, half-closing to the lid,
    Stares on OTRANTO's walls; grim terrors rise,
The horrid helmet strikes my soul unbid,
    And with thy CONRAD, lo! BIANCA dies.

Funereal plumes now wave; ALPHONSO's ghost
    Frowns o'er my shoulder; silence aids the scene,
The taper's flame, in fancy'd blueness lost,
    Pale spectres shews, to MANFRED only seen.

Ah! MANFRED! thine are bitter draughts of woe,
    Strong gusts of passion hurl thee on thy fate;
Tho' eager to elude, thou meet'st the blow,
    And for RICARDO MANFRED weeps in state.

By all the joys which treasur'd virtues yield,
    I feel thy agonies in WALPOLE's line;
Love, pride, revenge, by turns maintain the field,
    And hourly tortures rend my heart for thine.

Hail, magic pen, that strongly paint'st the soul,
    Where fell Ambition holds his wildest roar,
The whirlwind rages to the distant pole,
    And Virtue, stranded, pleads her cause no more.

Where's MANFRED's refuge? WALPOLE, tell me where?
    Thy pen to great St. NICHOLAS points the eye,
E'en MANFRED calls to guard ALPHONSO's heir,
    Tho' conscious shame oft gives his tongue the lie.

MATILDA! ah, how soft thy yielding mind,
    When hard obedience cleaves thy timid heart!
How nobly strong, when love and virtue join'd
    To melt thy soul and take a lover's part!

Ah, rigid duties, which two souls divide!
    Whose iron talons rend the panting breast!
Pluck the dear image from the widow'd side,
    Where Love had lull'd its every care to rest.

HYPOLITA! fond, passive to excess,
    Her low submission suits not souls like mine;
BIANCA might have lov'd her MANFRED less,
    Not offer'd less at great Religion's shrine.

Implicit Faith, all hail! Imperial man
    Exacts submission; reason we resign;
Against our senses we adopt the plan
    Which Reverence, Fear, and Folly think divine.

But be it so, BIANCA ne'er shall prate,
    Nor ISABELLA's equal powers reveal;
You MANFREDS boast your power, and prize your state;
    We ladies our omnipotence conceal.

But, Oh! then strange-inventing WALPOLE guide,
    Ah! guide me thro' thy subterranean isles,
Ope the trap-door where all thy powers reside,
    And mimic Fancy real woe beguiles.

The kind inventress dries the streaming tear,
    The deep-resounding groan shall faintly die,
The sigh shall sicken ere it meet the air,
    And Sorrow's dismal troop affrighted fly.

Thy jawless skeleton of JOPPA's wood
    Stares in my face, and frights my mental eye;
Not stiffen'd worse the love-sick FREDERIC stood,
    When the dim spectre shriek'd the dismal cry.

But whilst the Hermit does my soul affright,
    Love dies—Lo! in yon corner down he kneels;
I shudder, see the taper sinks in night,
    He rises, and his fleshless form reveals.

Hide me, thou parent Earth! see low I fall,
    My sins now meet me in the fainting hour;
Say, do thy Manes for Heaven's vengeance call,
    Or can I free thee from an angry power?

STELLA! if WALPOLE's spectres thus can scare,
    Then near that great Magician's walls ne'er tread,
He'll surely conjure many a spirit there,
    Till, fear-struck, thou art number'd with the dead.

Oh! with this noble Sorcerer ne'er converse,
    Fly, STELLA, quickly from the magic storm;
Or, soon he'll close thee in some high-plum'd hearse,
    Then raise another Angel in thy form.

Trust not his art, for should he stop thy breath,
    And good ALPHONSO's ghost unbidden rise;
He'd vanish, leave thee in the jaws of death,
    And quite forget to close thy aching eyes.

But is BIANCA safe in this slow vale?
    For should his Goblins stretch their dusky wing,
Would they not bruise me for the saucy tale,
    Would they not pinch me for the truths I sing?

Yet whisper not I've call'd him names, I fear
    His ARIEL would my hapless sprite torment,
He'd cramp my bones, and all my sinews tear,
    Should STELLA blab the secret I'd prevent.

But hush, ye winds, ye crickets chirp no more,
    I'll shrink to bed, nor these sad omens hear,
An hideous rustling shakes the lattic'd door,
    His spirits hover in the sightless air.

Now, MORPHEUS, shut each entrance of my mind,
    Sink, sink, OTRANTO, in this vacant hour;
To thee, Oh, balmy GOD! I'm all resign'd,
    To thee e'en WALPOLE's wand resigns its power.

History as "Retro":
Veiling Inheritance in Lennox's
The Female Quixote

Erin F. Labbie
University of Minnesota

> The effects of Romance and true History are not very different.
> > —Clare Reeves, *The Progress of Romance*

> Truth and appearances and reality, power . . . [woman] is—by virtue of her inexhaustible aptitude for mimicry—the living support of all the staging/production of the world. Variously veiled according to the epochs of history.
> > —Luce Irigaray, "Veiled Lips"

IRIGARAY'S claim regarding the mutability of the performance of "woman" cited in the epigraph above,[1] also calls into question a notion of performative aspects of history and, in so doing, signals key issues at play in a historiographical discussion of Charlotte Lennox's novel *The Female Quixote* (1752).[2] As I will argue in this essay, Lennox's protagonist, Arabella, exemplifies and enacts a process of mimesis which is in accord with Irigaray's formulation even while she demonstrates that process to be integrally tethered to a concept of history as contingent upon retrospective narratives.[3] Arabella's conflation of the historical romances that constitute and color her knowledge of her own contemporary eighteenth-century bourgeois life with "true history" foregrounds the extent to which romance and history are interdependent narrative genres. Blurring genre distinctions, such as they are, she posits a transgressive account of historical reality and challenges a concept of "distinct epochs of history"; as she performs the nobility of antiquity that is appropriated and fetishized by members of the eighteenth-century rising bourgeoisie, she concomitantly forwards a feminist poststructuralist approach to gender constructs. Through the mode of "retro" dress Arabella inscribes and reads "history" and "sexual difference" as semiotic signs of cultural performance, making visible a material gesture that calls attention to her status as a "woman" who is subject to, yet outside of, a specific and singular historical context. This play with temporality is hyperbolically present in *The Female Quixote*, a text where an intersection between sartorial and historical narratives performs a concept of "retro" history.

Through her appropriation of Old French romances, Arabella enacts those chivalric histories in the context of mideighteenth-century England, a context which has recently become a site for discussions of the creation of gender categories.[4] This pivotal moment in the history of sex and gender roles is generally understood to be due, partly, to a shift that occurred in the focus of the male scopic gaze. During the mideighteenth century, gender roles and constructs, previously maintained as social categories, became invested with a categorically ontological rigidity. The shift brought with it a new focus on female sartorial ornamentation and a commodification of fashion markers.[5] In other words, as women's ontological status began to inhabit their social status, making evident a collapse between interiority and exteriority, as well as surface and depth, which continues to be at work today, a perception of women as sites and objects of exchange began to be expressed through increasing commodification and distribution of fashion and its hygienic paraphernalia. Regarding this vestimentary change, Kaja Silverman notes that during the eighteenth century, "the male subject retreated from the limelight, handing on his mantle to the female subject," and that while male vestiture becomes uniform, "female dress and headpieces reached epic proportions."[6] Interestingly, amid this flux and construction of sexed identity, in *The Female Quixote*, Lennox's literary character Arabella already challenges this shift in the scopic gaze by paradoxically appealing to, and undermining, that gaze.

Attempting to emulate heroines of previous historical ages, whose success was largely dependent upon their actions rather than their appearance, Arabella's cross-historical dress is at once far simpler and more intriguing than the ornamental garb popular among the emerging bourgeoisie.[7] Significantly, her choice of dress places her in the realm of classical antiquity that was appropriated and evoked as the apex of culture in much Enlightenment scholarship. Lennox's gesture toward the Enlightenment trend to excavate, and perhaps exploit, classical ideals readdresses and critiques that trend. She casts her own glance back toward antiquity as she problematizes and satirizes what emerges as an idealistic nostalgia.

A consideration of "retro" risks exposing a similar nostalgia, and, indeed, looking toward the eighteenth century in order to locate a moment when "retro" is already being enacted and called into question, although its performance might seem to engage in the same antiquating process that seduced some thinkers of the eighteenth century. Yet, the complexity and paradox of Arabella's own "retro" dress and her concept of history rescue our own historiographical study from such repetitive pitfalls. For Silverman, "retro," the form of dressing that crosses "vestimentary, sexual, and historical boundaries," is a metaphor for the feminist postmodern project of drawing on the past to resituate that past within a contemporary setting:

> [Retro] inserts its wearer into a complex network of cultural and historical references. At the same time, it avoids the pitfalls of a naive referentiality; by putting quotation marks around the garments it revitalizes, it makes clear that the past is available to us only in a textual form, and through the mediation of the present.[8]

Silverman refers to "retro" as a mode of dress rooted in the 1960s, thus aligning it with the development of the "postmodern movement." However, for a consideration of gender constructs in the eighteenth century as they effect our own historical perception, it is highly significant that Arabella already enacts a "retro" style of dress in *The Female Quixote*. I suggest, therefore, that "retro" is not merely a postmodern manifestation of the second wave of feminism that revises social and ontological enlightenment symptoms, or residues, but, rather, is already located in Lennox's text.

If the phenomenon of "retro" dressing may be located in the eighteenth century (the historical moment most often cited by theorists and historians as the "origin" of scopophilia), then Silverman's argument assumes new historical implications for women who attempted to evade the commodifying and symptomalizing gaze even as they increasingly found themselves to be objects of its focus. At a time when, as Nancy Armstrong notes, didactic literature was the primary means by which women culled information on proper attitudes, style, and manners, Lennox demonstrates that through literature women may also discover subversive positions within society.[9] If we may consider "didactic narrative" as attempting to affect history by administering what a woman's desire *should* be—that is, by *advertising*—then the literature of the time is already controlling and commodifying female desire in a manner analogous to our contemporary capitalist fashion market. Arabella represents a fictional member of an historical culture who is bombarded by such texts, but one whose reading and whose politics remain innocent of that bourgeois dissemination of social expectations. In fact, if Lennox's own text may be, as it has been, read as a didactic treatise against the over-determined and over-invested reading of romances, then it may also be read as a satire on didactic treatises.

For Arabella, "retro" is the means by which she situates herself outside of the banal eighteenth-century bourgeoisie, and, ironically, attempts to reposition herself as a serious member of the sociopolitical realm. Although her cross-historical dressing is not always taken seriously by characters in the text, often making her the object of ridicule, Arabella's dress nevertheless makes socio-political statements about sex and class role expectations. Manifesting a desire to emulate heroines of antiquity, cross-historical dressing enables Arabella simultaneously to be the focus of attention and to subvert that focus. Indeed, her role demands a reconsideration of Silverman's notion of "retro" as an empty, acontextual gesture. Her ingenuous efforts to be taken seriously by everyone she encounters suggest that retro dress is not merely a vestimentary tactic that can be filled with any intention at any moment; rather, it is one that is invested with political participation and cultural ambitions. Arabella's dress is often described as striking precisely because it is more simple than the highly ornamental contemporary styles of eighteenth-century aristocratic culture.

Due to her reading, Arabella's concept of scopic attention assumes different expectations from those described by Lennox as popular in her society. Whereas, for example, Charlotte Glanville jealously competes with Arabella for the attention of Sir George, Arabella expresses a more liberated, even feminist approach to the attention of men. She would rather express herself and her ideas than participate in games that place matrimony and social escalation as the goal of male/female interaction.

In fact, in book 1.4–6, Arabella exhibits a strong sense of sisterhood, innocently supporting the morally questionable Miss Groves. Interested in the history of Miss Groves, Arabella convinces her waiting woman Mrs. Morris to narrate the interior workings of Miss Groves's soul, thus revealing her own perception of history as a narrative of the "thoughts of [one's] soul" as being derivative of personal experience (*FQ*, 78). Additionally, in book 3.5, "Some curious instructions for relating an history," Arabella instructs Lucy to tell her history. In response to Arabella's request, Lucy claims that "it is not such simple girls as I can tell histories; it is only fit for clerks and such sort of people, that are very learned" (*FQ*, 134). Demonstrating an utter lack of concern for a universalist historical account, Arabella, nevertheless, believes that Lucy is "learned enough." Lucy does not know how to write a history. She is not schooled in the attempt to link the chronicle with any form of singular truth. Therefore, encouraging Lucy to create and communicate a history of her life, Arabella shows her support for historical narratives that transgress any hierarchical structure. Arabella does not think that a divine relation between the subject and truth is necessary in order for an historical narrative to be considered valid. Rather, historical narrative is flexible and not bound to specific, stable, monolithic "Truth."

Arabella does, however, exhibit a concern with an empirical form of knowledge. Lucy is able to relate Arabella's history because she has witnessed the significant moments of her life. She has experienced the same events that Arabella would want communicated to others in the narrative formation of her public subjectivity. Without disregarding "events," this concept of history as a narrative process displaces a belief in history as recording a monolithic "Truth," forwarding an iterable, communicable sense of the past as it might affect the present. Arabella is interested in Miss Groves's history because she wants to understand Miss Groves's present state. She asks Lucy to relate her own history because she wants others to know her. Lucy's contentiousness, however, exhibits a more "enlightened" concept of history than that of Arabella since Arabella's monolithic historical narrative fails to represent the subject precisely because the fragmented subject cannot be reduced to a single narrative. Lucy's hesitancy, though appearing to be an issue of narrative authority based on a hierarchical concept of knowledge, points toward a more sophisticated approach to subjectivity as that which cannot be reduced to a single narrative. In this sense, Arabella's request for Lucy to recite her "history," similar to the practice of "retro," posits an ironic distance between origin and citation. Analogous to Arabella's approach to historical narrative, "retro" includes the past while undoing it, and recreating it. This process of citation and iteration maintains a trace of history while reinscribing it into the present, rendering "retro" metaphoric and metonymic for a

poststructuralist concept of the eighteenth century as that historical and literary period is construed as the origin and as the negation of its own construction. In Homi Bhabha's terms, Arabella's
retro dressing enacts a "metonymy of presence" that undoes the
histories she reads in the process of citing them.[10]

In book 7.7, "In which the author condescends to be very min-
ute in the description of our heroine's dress," Lennox provides a
detailed account of Arabella's dress, contributing to her text a
much needed dimension of materiality to the otherwise general
references to "the singularity of Arabella's dress." Ordering the
construction of a dress in the fashion of princess Julia's attire,
Arabella enters into a conflict with the dressmaker, who, lacking
her repertoire of historical romance, misreads her reference and
so cannot imagine princess Julia's dress. Only after an extended
discussion of fashion, and the dressmaker's frustrated surrender,
is Arabella's command executed by her own workwoman:

> "You can never persuade me," said Arabella, "that any fashion can be
> more becoming than that of the princess Julia's, who was the most
> gallant princess upon earth, and knew better than any other how to
> set off her charms. It may indeed be a little obsolete now," pursued
> she, "for the fashion could not but alter a little in the compass of near
> two thousand years."
> "Two thousand years, madam!" said the woman, in a great surprise:
> "Lord help us trades-people, if they did not alter a thousand times in
> as many days! I thought your ladyship was speaking of the last month's
> taste, which, as I said before, is quite out now." "—Well," replied Ara-
> bella, "let the present mode be what it will, I insist upon having my
> clothes made after the pattern of the beautiful daughter of Augustus."
> (FQ, 303)[11]

The scene reveals the fine lines between conscious and unconscious action that Arabella's dress subverts, as well as the effect of
her cross-historical dressing on Lennox's version of eighteenth-
century society. Deferring analysis of this passage for the moment,
however, it is important first to present the description of Arabella's appearance in order to provide a material foundation for
an analysis of the scopic and psychic effects of her appearance
on the public. Her adornment renders her performance one that
gestures toward the past while recontextualizing that past within
the present:

> She wore no hoop, and the blue and silver stuff of her robe was only
> kept by its own richness from hanging close about her. It was quite

open round her breast, which was shaded with a rich border of lace; and clasping close to her waist by small knots of diamonds, descended in a sweeping train on the ground. The sleeves were short, wide, and slashed, fastened in different places with diamonds, and her arms were partly hid by half a dozen falls or ruffles. Her hair, which fell in very easy ringlets on her neck, was placed with great care and exactness round her lovely face; and the jewels and ribands, which were all her headdress, were disposed to the greatest advantage. Upon the whole, nothing could be more singularly becoming than her dress; or set off with greater advantage the striking beauties of her person. (*FQ,* 303–4)

Challenging the contemporary style and material expectations, Arabella's cross-historical dressing inscribes the past into the present. Her precocity, then, suggests that "retro" and its cultural and historical effects are not merely responding to a concept of gendered identity that arguably originates in the eighteenth century, but also that the very historical space wherein this specific identity is created is also the space wherein it is deconstructed. Further, Lennox's tale, and Arabella's dress, as well as her approach to history (one that reads no difference between "real history" and "fictional history"), posits a historical and material account of history as "retro";[12] it undoes its own project by appropriating the past and recreating and resituating it into the present.

Reading history as "retro" calls for an approach to history similar to, yet more heterogeneous than, the one proposed by Mary Ann Doane when she claims that "the compulsion to repeat, based on forgetting, is a loss of temporal differentiation, the collapse of the past into the present" (*FF,* 95). This collapse of the past into the present does not merely erase the past; rather, it reinscribes the past into a present that is replete with history. That is, the past that returns to affect the present, returns, in a sense, from the future, and is real.[13] Although Arabella's cross-historical dressing does, on one level, attempt to erase the difference between past and present, its effects lend themselves to a theory of history as a reiteration and recreation of, rather than a simple collapse of, temporalities. She draws on fictional history to create her own present, therefore rendering that which has been marginalized as "fictional" history, true for her in the present. By engaging in retro dressing, Arabella enacts the reality of the fiction she lives.

Important to her complex representation of the past within the present is the fragile boundary between Arabella's conscious desire to dress like her heroines and the unconscious effects of that dress. Arguably, Arabella is attempting to uphold her notion of public codes by forming her dress according to her historical models of honor, respect, and authority, yet she remains largely unaware of the impression her dress evokes. "The surprise Arabella's unusual appearance gave to the whole company, was very visible to every one but herself" (*FQ,* 305). Nevertheless, her performance is highly integral to a reconsideration of the extent to which masquerade is unconscious and mimesis is conscious. At this point, Arabella's actions may be read to interrogate contemporary theory regarding masquerade and mimesis. Despite the complicated, highly conscious procedure by which her dress was finally made, Arabella does not become aware that she is the object of attention until the words "princess Julia" are "echoed at every corner."

Formulating her revisionary approach to the relationship between femininity and mimesis, Irigaray claims that woman must actively participate in a performance of the role of femininity in order to make visible the investment in that role as a means of "convert[ing] a form of subordination into an affirmation, and thus to begin to thwart it."[14] Her discussion of mimesis works to expose a secret past that was supposed to remain invisible. In order to find a means of empowerment and to exceed the role of subordination, Irigaray urges that women appropriate the very place of exploitation. For Irigaray, and, for Arabella, the exposure and disruption of modes of feminine exploitation are accomplished through citation and recitation of those very oppressive forces. By making visible the means by which the female subject is exploited, made the pure object of the scopic gaze, and commodified through that gaze, those means of exploitation are disarmed. In Irigaray's view, the performance of femininity must work to "make visible, by an effect of playful repetition, what was supposed to remain invisible." By gesturing toward the past as it is represented in her readings, we will see that Arabella takes Irigaray's project one step further: she exposes a past of subordination while enacting a possible past wherein women were not exploited and commodified. Arabella's historical process is integral, then, to an extension of Irigaray's call for subversion through recitation.

The deliberate assumption of the role of femininity enacted by Arabella, therefore, is already invested with her own theory and practice of mimesis. She seeks consciously to fulfill her own desire; and, yet, in order to perform the role described by Irigaray, Arabella must also remain unaware of the effects of her actions. Participating in the play of mimesis even while she remains elsewhere,

Arabella intermingles her conscious desire to appear as princess Julia with her unconscious desire to have an effect on the company at the ball. Despite, or because of, the foregrounded artificiality of her "natural" appearance, Arabella is more authentic than the other women of her class, and it is to this social/class anachronicity that they respond when they are taken aback by her self-presentation. The paradox of mimesis, then, as Arabella enacts it, proto-actively rewriting Irigaray's formulation, is that it must be both conscious and unconscious to be effective. Arabella must enact the past within the present, while forgetting the difference between the past and the present if her cross-historical dress is to be authentic and to subtly transgress her social context.

Arabella's engagement with mimesis, enacted through her "retro" performance, foregrounds an ironic distance between a fantasmatic origin of an object and its citation. Yet, central to the irony of her dress, are the effects her masquerade has on the public, which, to a large degree, remain unconscious.[15] This paradox might be rendered more comprehensible by looking to Nietzsche's observation that "wherever dissembling produces a stronger effect when it is unconscious, it becomes unconscious" (quoted in *FF*, 59). That is, when a conscious act is more effective in the public realm when it is perceived to be unconscious, then the act becomes incorporated into the subject's being to the extent that it assumes presence within the unconscious. Through repeated recitation and iteration of a gesture the construct of that citation—the quotedness of it—becomes "natural" or unconsciously enacted.[16] In order for the effects of her dress to be more effective, to appear more "natural" and more "real" in the public sphere, Arabella must incorporate her conscious desire to emulate her heroines into her seemingly unmediated actions.

Synthesizing conscious and unconscious actions reveals the connections between masquerade and mimesis, two concepts that are often thought of as having goals that are separate and distinct. Masquerade is perceived as an unconscious effect of dressing that enables one to "pass" for a member of a different social, historical, or sexual category. Mimesis, on the other hand, as we have seen here, is defined as that performance of subjectivity which must be assumed consciously. Arabella, incorporating conscious and unconscious effects of both strategies of self-representation, enacts what Diana Fuss, in reference to Frantz Fanon, has called "miming masquerade."[17] Dressing like her ancient and literary heroines, and yet, appearing to be purely unconscious of the effects of her dress, Arabella's miming masquerade has a double

and doubling effect: the mask and the process of masking become
a performance that involves the subject in a process of acting in
a scene where she plays the part of the subject playing the part
of the subject. In other words, Arabella's performance becomes
a metaperformance, always distanced from itself so that it may
reflect upon its own actions. In this way, the gesture and the act
being quoted become intertwined, miring any origin in the constant play and staging of the performance of performance. Similarly, Arabella's investment in appropriating the histories of her
heroines enables the past to become real within the present by
obfuscating any sense of a difference.

Interrogating the categories of surface and depth, the veil also
marks the difference between past and present, truth and illusion,
awareness and innocence.[18] However, the veil in Arabella's cross-
historical dressing does not merely break down these binary systems; it also demonstrates the way in which, at a crucial moment
in history—the mideighteenth century—the scopic gaze that is
shifting toward women is already being absorbed, as well as de-
flected, and reflected back upon itself. The crucial blending of
conscious and unconscious in Arabella's cross-historical "retro"
dressing demonstrates Lennox's stake in challenging the focus of
the gaze even as it is engaged in the process of formation. Lennox's text, therefore, exposes and problematizes the perception
of the eighteenth century as the moment when the gaze shifted
to posit women as the objects of that gaze, and the moment toward
which Silverman's conception of postmodern retro dress as subversive is directed.

In one of the first scenes in the novel (book 1.2), as Arabella
enters church on a brief reprieve from her castle, "making use of
the permission the marquis sometimes allowed her" to enter the
public realm, she blushes, feeling the gaze of Mr. Hervey. The
church is an integral space in this tale that criticizes and comments
upon the mobility of forms of historical narrative. Due to its overt
self-consciously historical presence (the church is always built to
represent the temporal other, or that which transcends time), it
manifests an architectural parallel to the "retro" character of Arabella's dress. As the church recapitulates and enacts the conventions of ritual and the Law of the Father, it makes its own form
significant. This presence of the Law of the Father in the church
affects the text on two levels: first, outside of the domestic space
of her home, the church is the only space where Arabella has her
father's permission "freely" to enter. In this sense, the church
serves as an alternate domestic space that is still controlled by her

father. Second, the church is ultimately enforced by God—the sovereign father.[19] Therefore, when Arabella enters the church, she enters an alternate private space that is, nevertheless, replete with the ritual and symbolic language of a public and historic culture. Within the church, contemporary issues are addressed within an antiquated setting and in the full disguise of convention and service to the past as it affects the present. Further, Arabella is veiled; she has "taken the veil,"[20] wearing her usual dress, which emulates her ancient heroines.

> Her dress, though singular, was far from being unbecoming. . . . Her headdress was only a few knots advantageously disposed, over which she wore a white sarsenet hood, somewhat in the form of a veil, with which she sometimes wholly covered her fair face, when she saw herself beheld with too much attention.
>
> This veil had never appeared to her so necessary before. Mr. Hervey's eager glances threw her into so much confusion, that pulling it over her face as much as she was able, she remained invisible to him all the time they afterwards stayed in the church. This action, by which she would have had him understand that she was displeased with his gazing on her with so little respect, only increased his curiosity to know who she was. (*FQ,* 8–9)

Despite Arabella's attempts to make herself invisible, her concealment only augments the focus of the gaze, provoking the desire of the Other to know her identity. In Fuss's words, for the Other gazing at the subordinated woman, the "veil functions as an exotic signifier, invested with all the properties of a sexual fetish" ("IC," 26). Her veil reveals in the act of concealing, thus placing her as "woman" in the visible realm of the very patriarchal culture that seeks to make her invisible.

As the gaze becomes more intense, Arabella's desire to shield herself also increases. However, despite the narrative commentary claiming that the veil covers her entire face, the language in this scene suggests that the veil is inadequate in completing its duty. "Pulling it over her face as much as she was able" illustrates that regardless of the extent to which her face is covered, she still needs to increase the degree to which she masquerades and performs her miming masquerade. She remains "invisible" only because she feels that her mask unilaterally conceals her self, failing to understand that in the act of concealing, not only does Arabella further attract Mr. Hervey's gaze, but, by tacitly communicating with Mr. Hervey via the veil, she reveals much about her ideals of courtly love and relationships between people within culture.

Feeling the violence of Mr. Hervey's gaze, Arabella seeks to prevent the imminent exploitation implied by the symbolization and
symptomalization (the process and expression of becoming and
making symptomatic) inherent in that gaze. As she pulls down
her veil, Arabella enters into the mimetic game by responding to
her vulnerability with an act of defiance, communicating her desire both to be respected enough to gain the right to distance
from the public (or, to be so visible that others must pretend that
she is invisible) and to enter a figural dialogue with Mr. Hervey.

Recalling my earlier discussion of Irigaray, one might say that
Arabella is making visible the desire to call attention to invisibil-
ity.[21] Reading Arabella's attempt to mask her face as a mimetic act
reveals her desire to be invisible in order to escape the realms of
the "perceptible" and the material. In an overdetermined manner,
Arabella hyperbolically submits herself to the realm of the perceptible in hopes of becoming so much a part of matter that she
is rendered invisible. Arabella, however, is not invisible to those
in the public realm; rather, she becomes more visible by calling
attention to herself as she actively veils her face. She makes visible
the act of becoming invisible and in so doing underscores a necessary connection between mimesis and masquerade.

Arabella's cross-historical dressing calls into question the difference between conscious and unconscious performances in a
manner that is parallel to Lennox's presentation of romance and
history as interdependent narrative processes. Writing a satire of
a woman caught up by the fictional lives of women in historical
novels, Lennox recreates such a fictional history as to draw the
reader into the text, interrogating the boundaries of history and
fiction. The material and the historical are bound up not only by
Arabella's retro dressing, but also, theoretically, by a discussion of
the veil and history that is illuminated in a context of Doane's
psychoanalytic analysis of the femme fatale in film. Presenting
history as that which is historical precisely because it refuses to
identically repeat itself, to mime itself, Doane posits a concept of
history as veiled, and without naming it such, as "retro." As in
Lennox's illustration and Silverman's analysis, Doane argues that
change occurs in history through a complex process of citation
and recitation. Explicating a relationship between psychoanalysis
and history that is integral to the present discussion of Lennox,
Doane argues that "for psychoanalysis, the past and present are
fully imbricated, locked in a struggle in which 'forgetting' is no
longer a simple accident, but a defensive weapon aimed against
the past"; while historiography, on the contrary, "solidifies its no-

tions about knowledge, power, and 'objectivity' by effecting a 'clean break' between the past and the present" (*FF*, 91). Attempting to fuse the two fields she otherwise defines as separate, she continues to argue for a psychoanalytic approach to historiography.

Although Doane's desire to render a psychoanalytic approach to historiography does effectively call for a reconsideration of the perceived differences between the two fields, her support of a "collapse of past and present" cited earlier in this essay simplifies the complex temporal relationship between past and present, and utterly elides the integral role played by the "future" in a psychoanalytic historiography. Merely to collapse these temporalities detracts from the complex dynamic of history in which past, present, and future are identifiable, but flexible: intertwined, yet affecting each other from outside of each other. Even within "retro," in which the past seems to become one with the present, that past is always being altered through a process of reinscription. To claim that a collapse or, on the other hand, a "clean break" occurs therefore obfuscates the narrative process to which history is subject. What needs to be accounted for is the persistent play of the past within the present, and the return of the repressed inscribing the future within a presence that is always available. This concept of history as retro that Arabella enacts is more aligned with Slavoj Zizek's discussion of the return of the repressed as coming from the future, and the notion, in his words that "we are all the time 'rewriting history,' retroactively giving the elements their symbolic weight by including them in new textures" (*SOI*, 56). In addition to recalling the interdependency of sartorial and historical narrative and performance, these "new textures" contain and represent the past while weaving that past into the present, rendering a new conception of the past. Parallel to the necessary play between the conscious and the unconscious, then, is the dynamic at play between history and theory, past and present. I suggest that, for this reason, "retro" style dress seems an apt metaphor for a process of historiography that is bound to a psychoanalytic perspective.

The material language that considers history a "texture," a "weaving," or a form of dress implicitly imbricates an analysis of history and sexual categories as narrative or discursive constructs. The relationship between Arabella's desire to veil her face, her self, and sexuality is demonstrated by a focus on her hair.[22] In the veil scene at church, the moment prior to the description of Arabella's headdress and attached veil focuses on the appearance of "artlessness": "Her fine black hair hung upon her neck in curls, which had so much appearance of being artless, that all but her maid, whose employment it was to give them that form, imagined they were so" (*FQ,* 9). Arabella's curls are contrived and manipulated until they appear to be natural, suggesting that their naturalness is constructed. The epitome of "femininity," that which is aesthetically beautiful and delicate, is revealed to be constructed to the extent that the very categories of sex and gender may be read also as constructed within culture. Arabella's "femininity" is a result of manipulation in a process parallel to that which conceives of history as empirically given truth. The ritual enacted by the maid who constructs Arabella's hair in order that it appear "natural" signifies the very ritual that history experiences as it is recorded in language. For history, this means that what is considered a "natural" or "essential" to historical truth is already constructed by the narrative that constitutes history.

Constructions of history and sexuality intersect during the scene in book 9.11, in which the doctor argues with Arabella in favor of historical truth as he attempts to undo what he perceives as Arabella's delusions. Considering the strong satirical nature of Lennox's text, this chapter, cunningly entitled, "Being, in the author's opinion, the best chapter in this history," and which has been read as the "real voice of the author," must also be read as satirizing the idea of stable truth.[23] Here, the doctor attempts to argue for real "Truth" and "History" as correlatives of fiction and history. Arabella's concept of history demonstrates an intermingling of the genres of truth and fiction, as well as empirical history and what is understood as narrativized history.[24] This of course is not a new observation; however, its place within Lennox's text renders it different from the generalized concept of relativistic history of poststructuralism. Rather than embody a purely relativistic theory, Lennox provides a tale that enables a perception of empirical truth, history, and fiction as overlapping, intertwined, and interdependent genres constantly in the process of being cited and recited. The doctor's argument centers on the premise that the texts Arabella reads as history cannot possibly be historical because they were written at a time that is distant from the moment of the recorded events:

"To prove those narratives to be fictions, madam, is only difficult because the position is almost too evident for proof. Your ladyship knows, I suppose, to what authors these writings are ascribed?"—"To the French wits of the last century," said Arabella.—"And at what distance, madam, are the facts related in them from the age of the writer?"—"I was never exact in my computation," replied Arabella;

"but I think most of the events happened about two thousand years ago."—"How then, madam," resumed the doctor, "could these events be so minutely known to writers so far remote from the time in which they happened?"—"By records, monuments, memoirs, and histories," answered the lady. (*FQ*, 415–16)

The doctor presents the notion that a real history must be written in a documentary, realistic style so that writing and action can coincide, thereby confirming the accurate record of the event. In this view, events need to be empirical by observed and personally witnessed for them to claim the authority of history. The doctor's is an approach which, as Arabella argues, is limited and illusory.[25] Her position is an intertextual one, suggesting that writing is produced in relation to other writings (i.e., "records, monuments, memoirs, and histories"). She does not directly challenge the idea about the occurrence of events; rather, she foregrounds the different possible media through which a concept of "contemporaneity" might be discovered, and, in so doing, she reconceives the very notion of "contemporaneity." As we read, textually we recall events, generating a present replete with a past.

According to the doctor's logic, only narratives that are written from a purely empirical, positivist perspective constitute history. His telos represents history as linear, finite, and eschatological. Revealing the doctor's opinion to be a fictional ideal, Arabella posits a concept of history as self-reflexive and self-disruptive, as a flexible entity that revises itself even as it cites itself. The doctor defines these different approaches to history according to sexual categories. Demonstrating Arabella's control to be within the symbolic realm, Patricia Meyer Spacks notes: "In Arabella's mythology, women absolutely control male destinies . . . she reverses the social convention that makes women compliant and dependent."[26] Threatened by this power, the doctor's motivation in "curing" Arabella may be perceived as a desire to prevent her from affecting the symbolic "masculine" realm. Pursuing his didactic argument, the doctor claims, "Love, madam, is . . . the sole business of ladies in romances" (*FQ*, 421).

Arabella's quixotic vision of a life in which love, honor, and intellect are the guiding principles is challenged by the doctor's empirical perception of a rational life which conforms to the patriarchal system. When the doctor claims that the "tendency of these books [romances] . . . is to give new fire to the passions of revenge and love," thus supporting the arguments that women should only read literature that will guide them to be better wives and socialites (i.e., the commodified didactic literature of the bourgeoisie), the subtext of his argument implies that the liberation Arabella finds in her chivalric world is contrary to the moral expectations of eighteenth-century England because it conflicts with rigid, dispassionate contemporary laws (*FQ,* 420). Patricia Spacks notes the emphasis on the polarities of "masculinity" and "femininity" in this scene, since Arabella demonstrates "feminine" characteristics, but emulates "masculine" values of honor and fame:

> The conflict played out by Arabella and the clergyman, between "feminine" emotionalism, fancifulness, and desire, and "masculine" rationality and piety, would recur, with the same gender assignments, most explicitly in the Gothic novel. Indeed, these gender assignments constitute eighteenth-century commonplaces . . . . Contemporary discourse on the male and female characteristics delineates a socially constructed opposition of qualities. (*DT,* 27)

Spacks's focus on the social construction of gender roles addresses the imposed nature of gender difference. By naming Arabella as the "feminine" emotional character in conflict with the rational "masculine" argument of the clergyman, she exposes the limiting nature of gendered and gendering narrative genres and paradigms of thought. Here, the feminine is aligned with a nonsensical, nonlinear approach to history, while the masculine is aligned with a rational, linear approach. But this scheme is, as I have argued, challenged by *The Female Quixote.*

Considering the confining role of sex categories inherent in definitions of history as linear and empirical or nonlinear and flexible, the reader may see the necessity for a concept of history that is tied to a material account such as the one proposed by this essay. Arabella's sartorial, historical, and exegetical mimesis reveals what Jacques Derrida describes in "The Double Session" as a performance of *reading* that involves mimesis and veiling: "The book, then, no longer repairs, but rather repeats, the process of spacing, along with what plays, loses, and wins itself in it. This, too, is literally to quote" (*D,* 235). Arabella's "retro" process of reading and quoting is dangerous to a culture that is attempting to interpolate women as commodified subjects precisely by administering to them didactic literature. Therefore, if Arabella's own form of didactic literature found in her reading of romances leads her to foreground the performance of reading through veiling, mimesis, and a miming masquerade, then she exposes and, in so doing, threatens, the very system by which the doctor's bourgeois culture defines order.

Ironically, serving as Arabella's teacher the doctor can only replace her within the very system of romance that he seeks to dispel. That is, by "proving" to her that her uncritical belief in the authenticity of the romantic histories she reads is not only false, but dangerous, he replaces her within a system wherein she submits to the bourgeois order, but also to the order of romance that he chastises. She marries Glanville and becomes a heroine of her own romance. The doctor's lesson, then, is that reading romances is dangerous to the mind and morality, but living them is crucial to the perpetuation of a certain mideighteenth-century class and order. In this sense, as Arabella's own quixotic performance exhibits, reading involves the subject in a constant process of "retro" engagement with the past, one that calls into question the very notions of past, present, and future that it iterates, interrogates, and inscribes.

Notes

1. Quoted in Mary Ann Doane, *Femmes Fatales: Feminism, Film Theory, Psychoanalysis* (New York: Routledge, 1991), 58; hereafter *FF*, cited in the text. The full section on "Veiled Lips" may be found in Luce Irigaray, *Marine Lover of Friedrich Nietzsche*, trans. Gillian C. Gill (New York: Columbia University Press, 1991), 118.

2. I would like to thank Greg Clingham, John Mowitt, Marilyn Mumford, Diana Fuss and the members of her seminar on the "Frontiers of Psychoanalysis," at the Dartmouth School of Criticism and Theory (1995) where discussion helped me to formulate many of these ideas regarding *The Female Quixote*, introduction by Sandra Shulman (London: Pandora Press, 1986); hereafter *FQ*, cited in the text.

3. On the history and play of mimesis from Plato to performance studies, see Jacques Derrida, *Dissemination*, trans. Barbara Johnson (Chicago: University of Chicago Press, 1981); hereafter *D*, cited in the text.

4. For discussion of gender constructs in the eighteenth century see, e.g., Thomas Lacquer, *Making Sex: Body and Gender from the Greeks to Freud* (Cambridge: Harvard University Press, 1990); G. S. Rousseau and Roy Porter, eds., *Sexual Underworlds of the Enlightenment* (Chapel Hill: University of North Carolina Press, 1988); Terry Castle, *Masquerade & Civilization* (Stanford: Stanford University Press, 1986); Randolph Trumbach, "Four Genders in the Making of Modern Culture," in *Third Sex, Third Gender*, ed. Gilbert Herdt (New York: Zone Books, 1994).

5. Roland Barthes's texts have been instrumental in semiotic analyses of these fashion markers. See esp. *Elements of Semiology*, trans. Annette Lauers and Colin Smith (London: Cape, 1967); *Empire of Signs*, trans. Richard Howard (New York: Hill & Wang, 1982); *The Fashion System*, trans. Matthew Ward and Richard Howard (New York: Hill & Wang, 1983).

6. For a more extended discussion of the scopic gaze, see Joan Copjec, "The Delirium of Clinical Perfection," *The Oxford Literary Review* 8 (1986): 61, 63, and Doane.

7. I say cross-historical dressing rather than historical cross-dressing because the former implies a difference of time and engages dressing that crosses historical epochs, while

the latter implies a difference of sex, and implies a cross-dressing the likes of drag, camp, etc. I must acknowledge, however, that in a sense the terms overlap by transgressing boundaries of sex expectations through time. I see gender-crossings and temporal crossings as intersecting and becoming interdependent. To cite difference within gender and time already places the performing subject in a position to disrupt and challenge categorical expectations.

8. Kaja Silverman, "Fragments of a Fashionable Discourse," in Tania Modelski, *Studies in Entertainment* (Bloomington: Indiana University Press, 1986), 139 and 150–51.

9. See Nancy Armstrong, "The Gender Bind: Women and the Disciplines," *Gender* 3 (1988): 1–23, esp. 12–16.

10. Homi Bhabha, *The Location of Culture* (New York: Routledge, 1994), 89.

11. I want to call attention here to the shift in class-power roles that emerges in this scene. The dressmaker becomes Arabella's teacher, attempting to impose rules and orders of etiquette expressed by the ornamental dress of the bourgeoisie and reveals her own dependence upon the commodification of fashion that also interpolates her into a capitalist system.

12. I perceive this concept of history as similar to Nietzsche's monumental concept of history. See Friedrich Nietzsche, "On the Uses and Abuses of History," in *The Untimely Meditations*, trans. R. J. Hollindale (New York: Cambridge University Press, 1983). However, it also includes the narrative process that enables the production and dissemination of that history. See Irigaray's *Marine Lover of Friedrich Nietzsche* for a more extensive theoretical and eloquent retrospective analysis of history and veiling in Nietzsche's oeuvre.

13. Freud discusses the "return of the repressed" in many places, such as *Beyond the Pleasure Principle*. Slavoj Zizek takes up Freud vis-à-vis Lacan, reinscribing the return of the repressed as it is narratively rendered a psychological process that is also material in its effects. "Retro" in its simplest form is precisely the past returning to the present as it is necessarily mediated by the future; see Zizek, *The Sublime Object of Ideology* (New York: Verso, 1989); hereafter *SOI*, cited in the text.

14. See Luce Irigaray, *This Sex Which Is Not One*, trans. Catherine Porter (Ithaca: Cornell University Press, 1985), 76. The passage I am presenting in somewhat of a bricolaged manner reads: "One must assume the feminine role deliberately. Which already means to convert a form of subordination into an affirmation, and thus to begin to thwart it. . . . To play with mimesis is thus, for a woman, to try to recover the place of her exploitation by discourse, without allowing herself to be simply reduced to it. It means to resubmit herself—inasmuch as she is on the side of the 'perceptible,' of 'matter'—to 'ideas,' in particular to ideas about herself, that are elaborated in/by a masculine logic, but so as to make 'visible,' by an effect of playful repetition, what was supposed to remain invisible: the cover-up of a possible operation of the feminine in language. It also means 'to unveil' the fact that, if women are such good mimics, it is because they are not simply reabsorbed in this function. They also remain elsewhere" (76).

15. Lennox reveals that mimesis must involve a certain degree of unconscious action and innocent intention or it becomes what Sir George and Charlotte enact, when they try to "capture" Arabella by mocking her style of dress and demeanor, and the scene ends in blood shed (book 7.11–13). In fact, Lennox illustrates the dangers of the cross-historical dressing that does not fuse conscious with unconscious, past with present. When Charlotte Glanville and Sir George decide to dress up as Arabella, hoping to trick her, their dress becomes camp, rather than masquerade or mimesis, suggesting that women can camp, a possibility that is questioned by many Queer theorists.

16. The example of epic theater perhaps not surprisingly has become a "classic" one in discussing this phenomenon of performativity, gesturing, and quoting. See Walter Benjamin, *Understanding Brecht*, trans. Anna Bostok (London: Verso, 1973).

17. See Diana Fuss, "Interior Colonies: Frantz Fanon and the Politics of Identification" (1994); hereafter "IC," cited in the text. Fuss notes that in recent feminist theory, masquerade is understood in opposition to mimesis. Her analysis of the veil in French-occupied Algeria fuses two apparently different approaches to concealment, rendering a "miming masquerade," in which the "mimetic act depends not upon excess but equivalency, not upon mimicry's distance from masquerade, but upon its approximation to it" (28). Fuss's analysis of masquerade and mimesis points toward a concept of the two that elides the difference between conscious and unconscious by claiming that their relationship depends on approximation to each other rather than difference from each other. Yet, she maintains the difference between the conscious effects of mimesis and the unconscious effects of masquerade. If the ironic difference and distance between the origin and the citation is to be subsumed beneath a purely convincing presentation of the self as the Other, whether that presentation crosses cultural lines, as in Fanon's text, or historical lines, as it does in Lennox's text, then conscious and unconscious must also be fused.

18. For a more extended discussion of the role of the veil in the surface/depth binary, see Doane on Nietzsche and Derrida in *Femmes Fatales.*

19. See Jacques Lacan, *Écrits,* on the Law of the Father, and the Symbolic and Imaginary realms as they might or might not pertain to reified spaces.

20. As Doane notes, "To 'take the veil' is to become a nun, to seclude oneself in a convent" (*Femmes Fatales,* 48).

21. For more on the reification and representation of the invisible in performance studies, see Peggy Phelan, *Unmarked: The Politics of Performance* (New York: Routledge, 1993).

22. The literary trope that foregrounds hair as the locus of artificiality is a pervasive one and one that is especially prominent in literature of the seventeenth and eighteenth centuries: most obviously in Pope's "The Rape of the Lock," whose heroine is also named by a derivative of Arabella (Belinda).

23. Even this consideration of the "real voice of the author" is a precarious one. The chapter has been attributed to Samuel Johnson. Although I have reasons for disagreeing with such attribution of authorship, given ambiguities of authorship, and given my discussion here of conscious/unconscious intent, perhaps the precise "author" is not so important.

24. See Hayden White, *The Content of the Form: Narrative Discourse and Historical Representation* (Baltimore: Johns Hopkins University Press, 1987) and White, *Tropics of Discourse: Essays in Cultural Criticism* (Baltimore: Johns Hopkins University Press, 1978).

25. For more on witnessing and memory, see Shoshana Felman and Dori Laub, *Testimony* (New York: Routledge, 1993).

26. See Patricia Meyer Spacks, *Desire and Truth: Functions of Plot in Eighteenth-Century English Novels* (Chicago: University of Chicago Press, 1990), 27; hereafter *DT,* cited in the text.

Sexuality on the Surface: Catholicism and the Erotic Object in Lewis's *The Monk*

Lisa Naomi Mulman
Duke University

IN his notorious Gothic novel, *The Monk,* Matthew Gregory Lewis leads us through labyrinthine corridors and caverns deep into the dungeons and crypts of our most powerful unconscious fears: fears of sexual deviance and domination, filial betrayal, and collapsed social hierarchy. The title character, Ambrosio, a sexually ravenous monk, guides the reader into a subterranean world where Satan can be summoned to work deeds of erotic terror, where unwary young girls are raped and entombed, and where behind the statues of virgins and saints lie the mute victims of hideous excess. Yet, the goblins and ghosts of Lewis's tale seem, after some investigation, more resistant to theoretical exorcism than such easy categorizations as those I just mentioned might imply. The conventional Gothic trope of the appearance of good as a screen for "hidden" evil would seem to lend itself to the Freudian model, with its emphasis on the repressed or "hidden" self. Freud's essential supposition that the self is divided into surface-level conscious and invisible (and repressed) unconscious spheres, as well as its assumption that pathology is residual in the interplay between the interior and exterior self, seems to cohere conveniently with the strategies of a late eighteenth-century writer such as Lewis, despite the real historical distance of over one hundred years between the most prolific writings of the Gothic period and the publication of Freud's seminal works.[1] Indeed, the potential for psychoanalytical interpretation of this and other Gothic texts, as well as the critical tradition that emerged in its wake, is persuasive enough to obscure the very significant cultural insights which might be gained by an interpretive strategy focusing on the drama which exists not in the psychologically symbolic network beneath the narrative, but in the discursive relations of the objects of the text themselves. Perched on the precipice of Freud's radical version of self-consciousness, *The Monk* is nonetheless a novel very much engaged with concepts of community and materiality that are not always amenable to the kind of inside/outside dichotomy suggested by Freud's model.

As Eve Kosofsky Sedgwick points out, the freeing of sexuality from such a critical matrix has profound implications for a more precise and, I would argue, more historically accurate apprehension of the novel. By deemphasizing the psychoanalytic, and necessarily more highly individuated nature of the attractions and repulsions of the text, Sedgwick paves the way for an interpretation of Gothic desire which is relational, ritualistic, and sensual: "In the Gothic view . . . individual identity, including sexual identity, is social and relational rather than original or private; it is established only ex post facto, by recognition."[2] Sedgwick uses the veils, mirrors, and faces of the text to establish the significant erotic charge of sensory recognition and its crucial role in the construction of a symbolic network whose meaning is residual not in what lies beneath the face (the "real" Ambrosio), but in the materiality of the face itself. Of course, the idea of a "symbolic" network without dimensionality is paradoxical; language is always significant. For the purposes of this paper, however, the value in examining the objects of the texts as objects of desire in and of themselves and apart from such signification is as a window into the important and ambiguous religious investments of the narrative. For, while Sedgwick focuses on the way in which object identities can be constructed through communal vision, I want to think about Lewis's use of such objects (precisely the veil, mirror, lamp, rosary, face) as sites of religious, aesthetic, and social anxiety rather than substitutive or fetishized sexual desire. This is not to say that the religious site is not an erotic site as well, but rather to locate that Eros as objective, self-contained, and potentially transcendent: interpretable, but not within the binary logic of traditional psychoanalytic theory.[3]

Reexamining the novel in these terms, a very different but equally compelling narrative pattern emerges. While Lewis, a Protestant aristocrat, appears, like his peer Anne Radcliffe, to vilify the Church through a depiction of carnal and corrupt monks and nuns, his actual (and quite profound) ambivalence toward Catholicism is manifested in the status of objects in the text, as well as in the nature and resolution of his various plot devices. Indeed, the objects affiliated with the Catholic characters and plots obtain the kind of sensual, communal status suggested by Sedgwick, while the Protestant characters and plots subscribe to a logic, indeed, an apprehension of events, which is quite clearly different. Unlike Radcliffe, who uses relics and Catholic personae only as foils for the establishment of ultimate and unquestionable Protestant hierarchical order, Lewis's narrative world includes (some might even suggest embraces) competing albeit dangerous and perhaps "immoral" visionary possibilities. The obvious anti-Catholicism of the novel is thus undercut by its presentation of a distinctly Catholic view of objects, a view which seduces the reader not only sexually, but more importantly, *sensually*. At the time of publication, criticisms were leveled at the text for its scandalous versions of sexual excess, which, even in the name of moral righteousness seemed extreme. In *The Pursuits of Literature*, for example, T. J. Matthias finds the novel, unlike many of its Gothic counterparts, "too important to be passed over in general reprehension" and containing "many poetical descriptions": "so much the worse again, the novel is more alluring on that account."[4] Matthias correctly recognizes the aesthetic quality of Lewis's evocations, and his extreme repugnance at the allure of the text reveals the true nature of anti-Catholic terror: the possibility that extreme investment in the material realm leads not to sanctification but to unchecked and unmediated impulse.

Of course, with indictment comes simultaneous fascination, and the novel titillates as much as it terrifies. This visceral reaction provides an emotional metaphor for the competing versions of reality offered by Lewis, one which textually affirms certain social conventions (the most important of these being proper marriage and its resultant domesticity), the other utilizing the communal structures and rituals intrinsic to Catholicism to interrogate the value and efficacy of such socially relational forms of identity in an increasingly unstable cultural climate. Although the narrative emphasis between these extremes is constantly slipping, a dichotomy can be discerned between what I will call the "Protestant" narrative, with its stress on domestic and constructed versions of events, and the "Catholic" narrative, wherein sensory apprehension of objects is primary.

Considering the emphasis on tradition and theological consistency inherent in the Catholic Church, I think it more salient than anachronistic to insert, at this point, a quotation from Dominican Robert Holcot, writing in the year 1349 on the Catholic stance on "images": "I worship not the image of Christ for that it is wood, neither for that it is the image of Christ, but I worship Christ before the image of Christ for it is the image of Christ which maketh me to worship Christ."[5] In other words, the site of desire is not (or not only) that which the image represents, but that which it *is*: the sensual, material representation of Christ. In this formulation, then, one would not have to invest in the whole theological "package" in order to evidence what might crudely be termed a "Catholic" sensibility. That this type of image worship exists in *The Monk* is evident throughout the text, most notably in the nature of Ambrosio's various unquenchable desires.[6] Ambrosio succumbs to the crafty Matilda, who we later find out is a messenger of the Devil. How does the Devil fashion his messenger in order to inspire lust in Ambrosio? In the image of the Virgin: "I watched the movements of your heart; I saw that you were virtuous from vanity, not principle, and I seized the fit moment of seduction. I observed your blind idolatry of the Madonna's picture. I bad a subordinate but craft spirit assume a similar form, and you eagerly yielded to the blandishments of Matilda."[7]

Surely it is, then, the image of Matilda as Madonna which makes Ambrosio long for her, and the Devil's exploitation of this impulse toward materially inspired passion to trap Ambrosio is, as it were, an effort to turn his own faith against him. Not accidentally, Ambrosio is regarded as the bastion of virtue in Madrid prior to this seduction, and his vulnerability to such an attack implicates not only Ambrosio but the entire monastic community (and, as we will later see, he is far from the only example of Church corruption in the novel). What is significant here, I think, is the way in which sensory perception and its companion, sensual experience, circumscribe Ambrosio's desire, and how these means of apprehension are inextricably linked to Catholic dogma. With this in mind, it is possible to understand Ambrosio's behaviors not as the repressed inner self breaking out, but rather as the outer self performing, albeit in an excessive way, the rituals of a specific social or communal context.

Importantly, then, Ambrosio's version of image worship works in tandem with sexual desire. Seeing, for him, becomes a material rather than an interpretive act, disorganized and tactile rather than ordered and normative. Ambrosio apprehends without ideology; his vision is perhaps narcissistic, as a child's, but it is not socially constructed, as is the Protestantly marked Alphonso's. Alphonso triumphs when, at the novel's end, he is capable of "seeing" the thin and disfigured Agnes as an alluring object, when he is capable, that is, of interpreting the "inner" or "secret" Agnes behind the material mask. What he is really "seeing" is, of course, the socially appropriate liaison he can now make with Agnes. Ambrosio's vision, on the other hand, is unconscious of social consequence and directed on the object itself: there is no "secret" subjectivity. The disjunction between the Freudian idiom and Catholic culture/practice becomes almost transparent here. Indeed, as Peter Benson has noted, for Freud the gaze always holds an implied judgment (and, by extension, I would suggest, an *analysis*). Writing on Freud's relationship to art, Benson observes:

> Freud himself was not immune to enthrallment to a work of visual art. Michaelangelo's statue of Moses, in Rome, had caused him to stand in front of it "every day, for three lonely weeks," a devotion at least as extreme as Dora's before the Raphael. For a time he was unable to remove himself from the scornful gaze of the prophet's large marble head, with its elaborately serpentine hair and beard. Under that implacable stare, Freud felt himself transformed into a guilty Israelite, caught cavorting round a golden calf.[8]

For Ambrosio, the effect of the painting is carnal, not moral, producing the sense that the Catholic monk sees without Freud's overlay of conscience. Freud's visual (and, not coincidentally, religious) icon holds tablets of law and language, while Ambrosio's is a depiction of maternal sensuality and nurturance.

Viewed in this way, the community of monks and nuns is subversive in the very fact that they are a community whose narrative is social and preverbal, resounding with literal and sexual "silences."[9] It is indeed interesting, then, that a text so concerned with the act of storytelling[10] should boast a villain so immune to the enticements of language, while simultaneously so susceptible to the allure of vision. When the unfortunate Agnes, a young novice who has transgressed and begged Ambrosio to conceal her crime, verbally attempts to activate his compassion, he responds, "Release me, I will not hear you!" (*M*, 48), only to later suffer some remorse upon *seeing* "the violence of her despair" (*M*, 49). Agnes's later fate will reveal the power of silence as she is secretly locked, pregnant, in a crypt to die of misery and starvation. Her rescue and restoration to order and domesticity is marked by her ability to narrate the course of events, to "tell." Similarly, Matilda, disguised as the young initiate Rosario, asks Ambrosio for his indulgence when she reveals the terrible "secret" that she is a woman and in love with him: "Oh, how I tremble to name the word! Listen to me with pity, revered Ambrosio! Call up every latent spark of human weakness that may teach you compassion for mine!" (*M*, 58). Ambrosio's response is a silent gaze which provokes a further explanation from Matilda, ostensibly designed to appeal to his virtue, not his libido: "What I feel for you is love, not licentiousness; I sigh to be possessor of your heart, not lust for the enjoyment of your person" (*M*, 59).

The test offered by Rosario/Matilda/Devil here refers precisely to the apparent separation between the virtuous inner "heart" and the lust-inspiring physical "person." Yet, as Holcot's comment demonstrates, Catholic worship deeply problematizes this dichotomy. Ambrosio cannot differentiate between the image which triggers his faith and that which triggers desire. Matilda recognizes this difficulty and narrates it:

> "Happy, happy Image!" Thus did she address the beautiful Madona; "'Tis to you that He offers his prayers! 'Tis on you that He gazes with admiration! . . . With what fervour He addresses his prayers to the insensible Image! . . . 'Tis Religion, not Beauty which attracts his admiration; 'Tis not to the Woman, but the Divinity that He kneels. Would He but address to me the least tender expression which He pours forth to this Madona!" (*M*, 80)

Matilda's words directly address the undercurrent of anti-individualism in this particular version of worship as they implicate Ambrosio in the love of "Divinity" (constructed as a broad, communal concept) not "woman" (the lower-case, individual woman that is Matilda herself). Indeed, Matilda's power to seduce Ambrosio is only solidified at the moment of visual revelation, and were she merely beautiful (such as Antonia, for example) she may not have served as the primary "seducing Object" (*M*, 78). As it is, his vision of her connects the entirety of his monastic training with his unrealized sexuality, a sexuality which is consistently directed toward the sacred Object: "Ambrosio sank back upon his pillow, and doubted whether the Object before him was mortal or divine" (*M*, 81).

I must emphasize that although it is the extremely fallible Ambrosio who succumbs to the temptations of Matilda, the conflation of sexuality and image worship is marked by Lewis as part and parcel of the Catholic community as a whole. Throughout the text, the site of sexuality is thus object-laden, configured by some combination of the rosary, the veil, the lamp, and the statue. Thus when Lorenzo first sees Antonia she is veiled and holding her rosary; when he looks upon her face: "What a Seraph's head presented itself to his admiration" (*M*, 11). Later, when Ambrosio enters Antonia's chamber in order to realize his profane desires, his image of her is illuminated by "a single Lamp, burning before the Statue of St. Rosolia" (M, 300). Similarly, when Lorenzo sees Virginia (who will later be the object of his affections) in the subterranean passages of the convent when "the beams of the Lamp darting full upon her face which was unveiled, Lorenzo recognized the beautiful Virginia de Villa-Franca" (M, 361). Significantly, this "unveiled" image of Virginia ushers in what will be the domestic (and Protestant) plot reconciliation where relationships are based on open, verbal affinity rather than physical enchantment. Shortly after seeing Virginia, Lorenzo discovers the hiding place of his victimized sister Agnes which has been concealed by a statue reputed to have "miraculous" qualities. Lorenzo disables the image in full sight of several of the nuns, who warn him of the dangers of "touching" the statue. Significantly, Agnes is punished for her sexual transgressions in a crypt hidden by the statue and containing only herself, her dead infant, and a rosary and crucifix. It is within a similar crypt that Ambrosio defiles Antonia, and this by the "pale glimmering of the Lamp" (M, 383). Likewise, the Bleeding Nun, image of sexual transgression and social displacement, holds a lamp, a dagger, and a rosary. Finally, and perhaps most importantly, Ambrosio, the personification of unchecked sexuality within the novel, drops his rosary early on, and the eager crowd, seduced by his eloquent presence, seizes it and divides it up into individual beads, each bead itself becoming an object of worship. This segmented rosary crystallizes the tension between the sanctity of the holy object (the rosary complete) and the possibilities for transcendence housed in each individual bead, thus providing an apt metaphor for the growing social conflicts between individually versus communally constructed versions of spirituality.

Another fascinating variation of this idea presents itself in the myriad of ways in which Lewis deals with images of veils and coverings throughout the novel. As many critics have pointed out, the veil, not only in this novel but in many British and American Gothic texts, exists as a metaphor for, once again, the "hidden" or repressed self or masked, enigmatic forms of desire, sometimes of a socially dangerous nature, and is naturally always linked to Catholicism.[11] But it is not only what the veil covers that provokes, but also the veil itself as an article that encapsulates both sacred chastity and its cousin, unholy desire. Indeed, it is easy enough to imagine, based on Lewis's evocation of the veil throughout the narrative, that the garment contains sensual power, both as covering and as object of desire. When, for example, Lorenzo first sees Antonia in church, her features are "hidden by a thick veil" (*M*, 9), yet he is drawn to her; the veil is a seduction as well as a barrier. This dynamic occurs continuously throughout the text as desire is provoked and deferred, gaining momentum through postponement. The veil thus obtains power as an article of this excruciating deferral, absorbing the force of passion into its very folds. In similar fashion, once Antonia lifts the veil and allows Lorenzo to gaze upon her, she does not return his gaze but displaces her passion onto her rosary: "She looked round her with a bashful glance; and whenever her eyes accidentally met Lorenzo's, She dropt them hastily upon her Rosary; Her cheek was immediately suffused with blushes, and She began to tell her beads; though her manner evidently showed that She knew not what she was about" (*M*, 12).[12] Antonia, the figure of female Catholic piety in the novel, is incapable of looking directly at Lorenzo and establishing a one to one relationship, choosing rather to mediate her desire through articles of faith, such as the rosary, and later, the Bible. Comparing this episode with Lorenzo's eventual relationship with Virginia, which is mediated through parental and sibling involvement rather than religious objects or imperatives, it is clear that such objects are disarmed by the domestic economy that Lewis establishes for Lorenzo and Virginia.

Underscoring the correspondence between objects desired and inanimate manifestations of passion are the qualitative similarities between them: Antonia's "dazzling white flesh" is very much like the veil which covers it.[13] Accordingly, rather than things of the text not being what they appear, they are, in at least one way, precisely as they appear, or, perhaps even more real than they seem. One of the more chilling incidents in Don Alphonso's story of his quest for Agnes is the tale of the Bleeding Nun: a ghostly unfortunate whose appearance thwarts rather than aids Alphonso in freeing Agnes from captivity. Unlike some ghosts, however, the Bleeding Nun is wholly convincing as a three-dimensional woman, managing to fool Alphonso into thinking that she is Agnes, even as he holds her in his arms: "She advanced to the spot where I stood. I flew to meet her, and clasped her in my arms. 'Agnes!' said I while I pressed her to my bosom. . . . Terrified and breathless She was unable to speak: She dropt her Lamp and dagger, and sank upon my bosom in silence" (*M*, 156). The animate object of desire and its inanimate correlative are, at least temporally, interchangeable. This lends credence to the notion that material apprehension is tantamount to passion—passion inspired from *without* rather than *within*. Similarly, Ambrosio's lust for Antonia coalesces as he views her undressing in Matilda's magic mirror:

> The scene was a small closet belonging to her apartment. She was undressing to bathe herself. The long tresses of her hair were already bound up. The amorous Monk had full opportunity to observe the voluptuous contours and admirable symmetry of her person. She threw off her last garment, and advancing to the Bath prepared for her, She put her foot into the water. It struck cold, and She drew it back again. Though unconscious of being observed, an in-bred sense of modesty induced her to veil her charms; and she stood hesitating upon the brink, in the attitude of the Venus de Medicis. At this moment a tame Linnet flew towards her, nestled its head between her breasts, and nibbled them in wanton play. The smiling Antonia strove in vain to shake off the Bird, and at length raised her hands to drive it from its delightful harbour. Ambrosio could bear no more: His desires were worked up to a phrenzy. (*M*, 271)

The mirror which allows him to view Antonia is also a barrier between them; he can look but is unable to touch. Nonetheless, it is through the mirror that the most erotic moment between them will occur. In this way the mirror takes on a sensual life of its own, and this sensuality is later transferred to the talisman which Ambrosio uses to open Antonia's door, and finally Antonia's body itself, which he violates without her consent and subsequently describes in wholly objectified terms: "He approached her with confusion painted on his countenance. He raised her from the ground. Her hand trembled, as He took it, and He dropped it again as if he had touched a Serpent. Nature seemed to recoil at the touch" (*M*, 387). Agnes, also, fixates her passion onto the inanimate as she clings to her dead baby in the crypt, as if it were a talisman or, more fittingly, a relic.

Yet it is not only the power of objects to encapsulate desire, but also to defer it, that strikes me as having particular religious resonance. Regarding the machinations of desire in the text, Wendy Jones has written: "When we consider the junctures at which the primary narratives intercept one another, a notable pattern emerges. Ambrosio's wishes are always gratified, while those of the good characters are continually blocked."[14] Suffering for love has a long and illustrious literary and religious history, and the two are oftentimes conflated, as they appear to be here. It is no accident that the virtuous characters must wait to have their desires filled, for there is value in waiting itself. Contrary to the narratives of religious mystics, however, the good characters in the text do not experience longing ecstatically, as some heretical Catholics (such as Ambrosio) might, but rather as a necessary step on the socially acceptable road toward the restoration of domestic harmony. Ambrosio brings on his own suffering, filling his desires with the knowledge that they are insatiable and that their temporary gratification is a form of mortification as much as pleasure. Unlike Alphonso and Lorenzo, he seeks (and obtains!) what he should not have, including, finally, his own sister. Alphonso and Lorenzo fix their desire on women who are within reach, socially and pragmatically, only to have circumstance intervene to delay the ultimate consummation of their wishes. The moral lesson offered by these twists of plot is residual in the antisensuality of the novel's happy ending: Agnes returns to Alphonso much altered after her confinement in the dungeon, and although she is restored to health, it is her deeper and more profound attachment to her lover which truly reunites them: "These once passed, the tranquillity of his mind, the assurance of felicity, and above all the presence of Agnes, soon enabled him to overcome the effects of his late dreadful malady. The calm of his soul communicated itself to his body, and He recovered with such rapidity as to create universal surprize" (M, 400). Likewise, Lorenzo's relationship with Virginia develops slowly, and as friendship: "His relations, as well as the Lady, perceived that with every day her society seemed to give him fresh pleasure, and that He spoke of her in terms of stronger admiration" (M, 401). The trials which Lorenzo and Alphonso endure lead them to depths of feeling inspired by virtue and affection rather than erotic attraction, enforcing the importance of social propriety and a religiosity which is dependent upon such domestic order; domestic rather than spiritual rituals constitute the story's "happy ending."

But what of the other, uncanny and horrific ending, the fate of Ambrosio? Unlike Radcliffe, Lewis does not capitulate to the forces of reason and offer a rational explanation for the "supernatural" events of the narrative. Rather, he acknowledges the presence of the Devil, and allows him to supervise Ambrosio's ruin, casting aspersions on the companion "happy" ending by introducing the possibility that Protestant domestic order, while apparently triumphant, is not singular—the Devil's logic, Ambrosio's logic, and, in the context of the narrative, Catholic logic, exist as well. Likewise, because Ambrosio is a monk, the narrative implicitly recognizes the intimate relationship between certain types of religious passion and the power to alter or transform circumstance, sometimes in a subversive manner. Matilda's dual identity as a chaste male monk and a powerful female sorceress underscore this point; good and evil are interchangeable in the Ambrosio/ Matilda power economy, whereas only virtue obtains in the Lorenzo/Alphonso plot line. The Devil (in the guise of Matilda) can thus transform the good (Ambrosio) into the ultimately bad: the incestuous rapist/murderer who has transgressed in every possible way. In another variation on this theme, Antonia "sees" Ambrosio as a savior rather than a villain and persists in this vision even after he has murdered her mother and attempted to rape her. The reality of Ambrosio, like that of Matilda, is mutable as well as circumstantially subjective. In such a world, it would seem, virtuous behavior is always susceptible to interference, and the source of such interference is always in the realm of excessive, untempered passion. Thus Ambrosio's sensual passions destroy him, and his final fear of bodily agony results in his selling his soul, the ultimate exhibition of the priority of materiality in the narrative. Indeed, Ambrosio's demise is characterized by physical pain:

> The Sun now rose above the horizon: Its scorching beams darted full upon the head of the expiring Sinner. Myriad's of insects were called forth by the warmth; They drank the blood which trickled from Ambrosio's wounds; He had no power to drive them from him, and they fastened upon his sores, darted their stings into his body, covered him with their multitudes, and inflicted on him tortures the most exquisite and insupportable. The eagles of the rock tore his flesh piecemeal, and dug out his eye-balls with their crooked beaks . . . six miserable days did the Villain languish. (M, 442)

Once again, the novel demonstrates the dual nature of religious energy. Ambrosio suffers six days and expires on the seventh; as God created the world and rested, so does the Devil do his work.

Ambrosio does not exercise reasonable compassion, as Agnes implores, but rather works miracles—miracles of evil. The slippage inherent in this dichotomy, at least as evidenced in this novel, performs a critique of Catholicism which primarily implicates not the hierarchical structure of the Church (and I would argue that Lewis is finally an advocate of hierarchy), but rather its overriding sensibility, its emphasis on material manifestations of religious fervor and the vulnerability of such manifestations to excess and sexual displacement. The power of objects, whether they be animate (such as Antonia) or inanimate (like the veil), to stimulate, transform, and embody passion is anxiety-provoking for the narrator, who seems to recognize a social and moral threat in such allurements. While it is imprecise to ascribe the type of materiality I have here outlined to a specifically Catholic theology, such materiality is clearly an element of Catholic worship and a contributor to larger cultural (and admittedly stereotyped) understandings of Catholic sensibility. This was especially true at the time of Lewis's writing, when anti-Catholic sentiment was aimed quite clearly at the physical pomp and circumstance of the Roman Church, as well as the sexual corruption of its members. And lest we fall victim to the trap offered by scholars who fail to place such eighteenth-century issues along a historical continuum stretching clearly into the nineteenth century and beyond, I offer this quotation from a famous practitioner of the American Gothic:

> Here was a priesthood, pampered, sensual, with red and bloated cheeks, and carnal eyes. With apparently a grosser development of animal life than most men, they were placed in unnatural relation with women, and thereby lost the healthy, human conscience that pertains to other human beings, who own the sweet household ties connecting them with wife and daughter."[15]

Ambrosio's "carnal eyes" constitute a way of seeing and desiring in *The Monk* which, while set over and against the "sweet household ties" of the Protestant ending, does not fully eradicate its persuasiveness. Ironically, Lewis's achievement in *The Monk* is the creation of a narrative which ultimately celebrates the mysteries of the flesh, combining condemnation with fascination to suggest contradictions reconcilable only through faith.

Notes

1. The lectures which were to become the published volume *Introductory Lectures in Psycho-Analysis* were first delivered in 1916–17; *Beyond the Pleasure Principle* was published in 1920, *The Ego and the Id* in 1923, and *The Interpretation of Dreams* made its first appearance, in German as *Die Traumdeutung,* in 1899.

2. Eve Kosofsky Sedgwick, " The Character in the Veil: Imagery of the Surface in the Gothic Novel," *PMLA* 96 (1981): 256.

3. Indeed, Freud himself feels the need to account for the power of the visual to disable or alter the psychoanalytic process. Perhaps the most striking example of this occurs during his famous case study of the hysteric Dora whose rapt and inarticulate stance before the Sistine Madonna provokes Freud to narrate the incident as the fetishized response to the vague outlines in the background of the painting and their resemblance to the obscured female genitalia. What Freud fails to account for is, predictably, the possible religious elements of the episode. The painting is, after all, a representation of the Madonna. See Sigmund Freud, *Fragment of an Analysis of a Case of Hysteria,* Standard Edition of the Complete Psychological Works, ed. James Strachey, 22 vols. (London, 1953–74), 7:96.

4. T. J. Matthias, *The Pursuits of Literature*, 13th ed. (London: Becket, 1805), 245, 248, 249.

5. Quoted in G. R. Owst, *Literature and the Pulpit* (Oxford: Oxford University Press, 1961), 143.

6. I must add here that the theological significance of the image debates cuts directly to the heart of British anti-Catholic paranoia during the seventeenth and eighteenth centuries, when churches and cathedrals (including the relics therein) were routinely destroyed and recreated as a means of instituting an atmosphere of worship unmediated by material representations of the sacred.

7. Matthew Lewis, *The Monk* (Oxford: Oxford University Press, 1973), 440; hereafter *M*, cited in the text.

8. Peter Benson, "Freud and the Visual," *Representations* 45 (1994): 101.

9. In *Agnes of Sorrento*, Harriet Beecher Stowe acknowledges this with sympathetic condescension: "The rosary, the crucifix, the shrine, the banner, the procession were catechisms and tracts invented for those who could not read, wherein the substance of pages was condensed and gave itself to the eye and touch. Let us not, from the height of our day, with the better appliances which a universal press gives us, sneer at the homely rounds of the ladder by which the first multitudes of the Lord's followers climbed heavenward." See Harriet Beecher Stowe, *Agnes of Sorrento* (Boston: Houghton Mifflin, 1896), 96–97.

10. See Wendy Jones, "Stories of Desire in *The Monk*," *ELH* 57 (1990): 129–50, for an interesting account of the importance of competing narratives in the text.

11. An excellent example of this can be found in Jenny Franchot's analysis of Nathaniel Hawthorne's story "The Minister's Black Veil": "Hawthorne's tale of a Connecticut minister's enigmatic decision to live life shrouded in a black veil exploits the growing fascination with the secrets of Catholicism and, more particularly, as shown by the Ursuline riot, with the potentially incendiary provocations of the veiled." See Jenny Franchot, *Roads to Rome: The Ante-bellum Protestant Encounter with Catholicism* (Berkeley: University of California Press, 1994), 221.

12. This type of displacement has a particular and notable resonance for psychoanalysis, especially as the "interiority" of Freudian theory is examined against models such as the one I am proposing in this essay. I am thinking specifically of Sander Gilman's account of Freud's nursemaid's attempt to convert him to Catholicism using a rosary, a conversion attempt which the adult physician Freud would recontextualize as an effort to sexually seduce rather than religiously convert him. Freud's sexualization of the scene and the object involved (the rosary) is significant, in Gilman's view, because it demonstrates Freud's (hyper) awareness of his Judaism and his desire to understand his religious "otherness" as universal sexual vulnerability. Lewis reverses Freud's impulse by locating sexual desire in the religious object, "othering" the Catholic by localizing his desire. See Sander Gilman, *The Case of Sigmund Freud* (Baltimore: Johns Hopkins University Press, 1993).

13. This is particularly exemplified by the figuration of the veil as object which is desired both for its own tactile qualities as well as for that which it obscures. Indeed, the veil and other such objects take on this peculiar dual status as things which both represent desire and are themselves desired. As Eve Sedgwick writes: "Like virginity, the veil that symbolizes virginity in a girl or a nun has a strong erotic savor of its own, and characters in Gothic novels fall in love as much with women's veils as with women" ("The Character in the Veil," 256).

14. Wendy Jones, "Stories of Desire in *The Monk*," 135.

15. Nathaniel Hawthorne, *The Marble Faun; or, The Romance of Monte Beni* (Columbus: Ohio State University Press, 1968), 411.

Violence against Difference: Mary Wollstonecraft and Mary Robinson

Adriana Craciun

Loyola University, Chicago

WOMEN'S violence transgresses the boundaries that establish both sex and gender like no other act can—not only are such women not properly feminine, but they cease to be female.[1] Women's violence was for many the most shocking of all the French Revolution's bloody excesses, simply because the actors were women; even Sade found Charlotte Corday's assassination of Marat disturbing: "Marat's barbarous assassin, like those mixed beings whose sex is impossible to determine, vomited up from hell to the despair of both sexes, directly belongs to neither."[2] Images of Charlotte Corday and of the mobs of armed, enraged Parisian women are still with us today, a testament to their power to disturb our lingering concepts of women as inherently nonviolent. Because such violent women are typically described as bestialized or at least as unsexed, it is too often assumed that such descriptions serve only misogynist ends and are found largely in the works of men. Yet because the violent woman violates both the limitations and the virtues of natural womanhood so spectacularly, she is necessarily of interest to us today when feminism's identity, grounded in the problematic existence of "woman," is in crisis.

In exploring British women writers' representations of such violent women, we need to avoid two dangers of interpretation. The first is that these images of aggressive women represent and celebrate unbridled female agency and power. The second, equally dangerous, position is that these images of aggressive women are simply products of male misogyny internalized by women. Each perspective is insufficient, but together they produce a constructive tension that I will focus on throughout this essay. In an important sense, my project is in a similar double-bind as were late eighteenth-century women: Madame de Staël wrote that women's "destiny resembles that of freedmen under the emperors: if they try to gain any influence, this unofficial power is called criminal, while if they remain slaves their destiny is crushed."[3] The autonomous, stable female subject outside history and solely in a negative relationship to power is not, however, the elusive object of this study. Rather, a feminist Foucauldian approach to this double-bind is, I believe, most productive, for the modern subject as both effect and agent of power is most spectacularly illustrated by the violent female subject. As the embodiment of this unresolvable contradiction of women's agency as both produced by and resistant to power, the violent woman manifests this tension on a corporeal as well as subjective level. For the violent female body, like the subject, neither eliminates its natural corporeal limitations through its violence, nor leaves them intact, but, most significantly, foregrounds their construction and instability.

The mutability of "natural" boundaries which the violent woman foregrounds is best understood if placed in its revolutionary historical context, for such mutability was indeed revolutionary. "During the French Revolution," writes Lynn Hunt, "the boundaries between public life and private life were very unstable." Following the official expulsion of women from the public sphere in 1793, "this line between public and private, men and women, politics and family, became more rigidly drawn."[4] French women's struggle to redefine women's sphere, women's rights, and women themselves during this brief period of radical disorder has been the subject of excellent scholarship in the last decade. Drawing upon these accounts of French women's revolutionary activism, I will examine British women's responses to and characterizations of this uncommonly tumultuous period in women's history. Hunt's focus on "the unstable boundaries of the French Revolution" serves as an excellent starting point for my own inquiry, for I will also examine unstable boundaries—boundaries between masculine and feminine, between male and female, and between the two categories—"cultural" and "natural"—themselves.

The French Revolution and Women

Madelyn Gutwirth concurs with Lynn Hunt and other feminist historians that revolutionary representations of Woman as Liberty, Republic, Maenad, and Mother Nature did not reflect women's power in revolutionary society, but, rather, marked its absence, and ultimately reinscribed male sex-right and misogyny. The "radical Revolution ratified, rather than challenged, male sex-right. This is largely because the French Revolution itself arrived in the midst of a longer and broader struggle to resist women's advancement in society."[5]

This struggle for women's advancement connects British women of the Romantic period to their French counterparts. Yet women's own representations of such violent revolutionary women are left largely unexamined in both Hunt's and Gutwirth's accounts. Are women's Maenads examples of their internalization of male misogyny? Do images of violent and destructive women serve men's interests in maintaining women's oppression? Were the images in question found solely in the works of men, it would be easier, though still not unproblematical, to answer the last question in the affirmative. Yet once one has begun to see similar images in the works of women, any certainty about the uniform functions of these images, as either misogynist demonizations or feminist celebrations, begins to appear unfounded.

Women and men did not, for the most part, use these images with identical political interests, yet such political differences occurred not merely between men and women, but also within each gender category, especially according to class. The difficulty in aligning women's and men's political interests in the revolutionary period, both in England and France, has been explored by scholars such as Joan Landes. Olympe de Gouges, probably the most radical feminist of her day, author of the remarkable *Declaration of the Rights of Woman,* was a monarchist. Mary Robinson, a well-known British republican and a radical feminist, wrote a sentimental apotheosis of Marie Antoinette[6] that Burke himself would have been proud to write.

Joan Landes makes a powerful case for such asymmetry in men's and women's political interests vis-à-vis the Revolution, arguing that because the new "Republic was constructed against women, not just without them,"[7] class interest often prevailed over that of gender for women. French women's public presence and influence in cross-class salons during the *ancien régime* remained attractive to elite women faced with the new bourgeois public sphere and its demonization of masquerade, performance, wit, stylized speech, luxurious dress—in short, of all things feminine. Under the new doctrine of universal rights, however, women could only be included if effaced by the male universal, or claim lesser rights and greater moral authority under the sign of differ-

ence and exclusion from the universal, which most women ultimately did.

British women's experience parallels this gendering of the public sphere in France and was influenced by it. Katharine Rogers
writes that English male and female observers of the eighteenth
century were struck by precisely the "feminine" elements of the
ancien régime discussed by Landes, and imagined French women to
have great influence over political and personal matters through
their mastery of witty conversation, flattery, sexual favors, fashion,
and affectation. Women such as Elizabeth Montagu and Wollstonecraft celebrated this mingling of the sexes in the public space
of the salon, though other British women, such as Frances Burney
and Maria Edgeworth, had more reservations regarding French
women's relative sexual and intellectual liberties.[8] Thus, the unstable boundaries of the French revolutionary period, destabilized
in part by French women's radical and highly visible activism,
provide an excellent context in which to trace British women's
representations of women who exist between these boundaries of
public/private, masculine/feminine.

This paper will explore British women's representations of
women's sexed bodies as constructed and mutable, focusing on
the debate in the 1790s over the nature and history of women's
physical strength. While most feminist theorizing of the body has
focused on maternity, sexuality, hunger, or disease, I have inten-
tionally limited my discussion of sexual difference to strength,
leaving these more familiar areas untouched. I have done this
in order to isolate strength from sexuality and maternity as an
independent category, a category which these women themselves
isolated and distinguished as an area of possible mutability. While
women such as Wollstonecraft critiqued the deleterious effects of
maternity as women's sole social outlet, they didn't question the
centrality of maternity to female experience, which is understandable given the social centrality of maternity to women's lives in the
late eighteenth century. My focus on corporeal strength is not
intended to detract from the significance of maternity and sexuality in studies of the sexed body; it is instead intended to draw
attention to an overlooked, yet central, dimension of the history
of the sexed body and of modern feminism.

> Why may not woman resent and punish?
> —Mary Robinson

"The question is simply this," wrote Mary Robinson in 1799:
"Is woman persecuted and oppressed because she is the *weaker*

creature?"[9] Robinson poses her rhetorical question about the history and mechanism of women's subordination—their supposed weakness—on two levels, mental and physical. Her essay, *A Letter to the Women of England, on the Injustice of Mental Subordination,* deals with both mental and physical subordination, though this corporeal dimension of early feminism's struggle has typically been overlooked, as it was left out of Robinson's own title. Early feminism's critique and revision of physical sexual difference marks a crucial step in the history of the construction of the domestic female body as maternal, yielding, receptive, yet always dangerously susceptible to sexual disorder and excess.

Though feminists such as Wollstonecraft, Robinson, Macaulay, and Williams used the liberal discourse of universal rights and reason to give women equal access to this regime of reason, they always simultaneously addressed the role of the body in the construction of gender. In fact, these writers suggest that it is not only women's characters, intellect, and manners which need revolutionizing, but also their bodies and bodily limitations. The answer Robinson suggests to her own question is no, women are the weaker sex because they are subordinated and their bodies disciplined: "Let WOMAN once assert her proper sphere, unshackled by prejudice and unsophisticated by prejudice; and pride, (the noblest species of pride,) will establish her claims to the participation of power, both mentally and corporeally" (*LWE,* 2).

Robinson's essay, despite its title, is primarily concerned with women's physical capabilities, responses, and limitations, as they relate to their subordinate social status. "[T]he prominent subject of my letter," writes Robinson, is "that woman is denied the first privilege of nature, the power of SELF-DEFENCE" (73):

> Supposing that a WOMAN has experienced every insult, every injury, that her vain-boasting, high-bearing associate, man, can inflict: imagine her, driven from society; deserted by her kindred; scoffed at by the world; exposed to poverty; assailed by malice . . . ; she has no remedy . . . . She talks of punishing the villain who has destroyed her: he smiles at the menace, and tells her, *she is,* a WOMAN. (*LWE,* 7–8)

This description of women's condition, like Wollstonecraft's *Maria, or The Wrongs of Woman,* locates the fictional conventions of the persecuted heroine popular in late eighteenth-century fiction in women's historical position respective to male law, institutions, and, especially, violence. Richardson's Pamela exemplifies this embattled heroine, and Pamela herself best expresses the widespread belief that women's strength lies in their physical weakness:

> I . . . have reason to bless God, who, by disabling me in my faculties, empowered me to preserve my innocence; and, when all my strength would have signified nothing, magnified himself in my weakness.[10]

Robinson's response to the deplorable condition of this victimized woman is to rouse her from her learned passivity by drawing attention to her body and its self-imposed limitations: "Why may not woman resent and punish? Because the long established laws of custom, have decreed her *passive!*" (*LWE*, 8).

Robinson rewrites the ubiquitous seduction plot by offering a counterexample that rejects the equation of women's strength with weakness. When her lover attempted to seduce her before their marriage day, the lady in Robinson's example[11] met him at their romantic rendezvous armed with pistols and a challenge:

> "Remember for what infamous purpose you invited me here: you shall never be a husband of mine; and such vengeance do I seek for the offence, that, on my very soul, you or I shall die this hour. Take instantly up the pistol, I'll give you leave to defend yourself; though you have no right to deserve it. In this, you see, *I* have honour, though *you* have none." (*LWE*, 22)

The lady's statement draws attention to the disparity between male and female honor, and she claims the right to both kinds—she maintains her chastity (women's honor) by actively defending it in a duel, the quintessential test of male honor. Though (or rather, because) the lover tried to calm the lady using "soft phrases" and blamed her beauty as the cause of his seduction, "she shot him through the heart" (*LWE*, 23). "This short story will prove," writes Robinson, "that the mind of WOMAN, when she feels a correct sense of honour, even though it is blended with the very excess of sensibility, can rise to the most intrepid defence of it" (*LWE*, 25). Robinson in fact rewrites the seduction plot from *Clarissa* onwards, insisting that women enlarge their understanding of honor and take up arms to actively defend it and themselves.[12] Robinson also extends Wollstonecraft's similar call for "a manly spirit of independence" in *Vindication of the Rights of Men*[13] to women, and indeed, Robinson saw her essay as a continuation of Wollstonecraft's republican feminist program, calling herself a member of a whole "*legion of Wollstonecrafts.*"

The right to resent and punish is rarely claimed by feminists of the 1790s, since it challenges women's moral superiority and benevolence which was increasingly seen as grounded in the middle-class maternal body. Yet for Robinson the question of how women's bodies are constructed as feminine because they are weaker is central to the problem of their continued political subordination; if men's oppression of women were understandable given their "natural" superiority in strength, she argues, then women who are physically stronger than men should likewise be able to oppress men:

> In what is woman inferior to man? In some instances, but not always, in corporeal strength: in activity of mind, she is his equal. Then, by this rule, if she is to endure oppression in proportion as she is deficient in muscular power, *only*, through all the stages of animation the weaker should give precedence to the stronger. Yet we should find a Lord of the Creation with a puny frame, reluctant to confess the superiority of a lusty peasant girl, whom nature had endowed with that bodily strength of which luxury had bereaved him. (*LWE,* 17)

Robinson argues that since some women are stronger than some men, relative strength and weakness are found along a continuum, not necessarily according to sexual difference. Robinson also critiques class and gender as constructs (as Wollstonecraft did in *Rights of Woman* [1792]): luxury and idleness shape the body of the wealthy man, much as labor does that of the "lusty peasant girl." These constructions of peasant and aristocratic body in turn shape the constructions of those classes of subjects, one thought to require a higher standard of living, the other to be able to bear harsher conditions without harm.

The right to aggressive self-defense, argues Robinson, without being labeled debased and "unwomanly," would mean the end of woman as weakness. Robinson reminds women that they perform the most difficult and laborious physical chores without anyone thinking twice that they may be too weak for such drudgery. Instead of being the cause of women's mental and political subordination, she argues, women's supposed physical weakness is actually the effect of that subordination. Women's natural difference (i.e., their inferior strength) is thus an *effect* of gender, to apply Judith Butler's argument, so that "gender is not to culture as sex is to nature; gender is also the discursive/cultural means by which 'sexed nature' or 'a natural sex' is produced and established as 'prediscursive.'"[14] Chris Cullens, in "Mrs. Robinson and the Masquerade of Womanliness," also connects Butler's model of performative gender to Robinson, saying of her novel *Walsingham* that it "represents, in Butler's words, a partial 'exposure of the rift between the phantasmatic and the real whereby the real admits itself as phantasmatic.'"[15]

The body of woman as weakness, hence the body of a "real woman," is revealed as phantasmatic not only in works of feminists who urged women to surpass the identity of woman as weakness but, as we shall see, also in works of conservative writers who urged submission to the physical inferiority ascribed to women within the ideology of sexual difference. Both conservative and progressive thinkers of the period knew that disciplining the body and controlling its practices simultaneously materialized both political subjects and politicized bodies. Feminist criticism needs to acknowledge this problematic status of the female body even in the late eighteenth century when the cult of proper femininity had such force, and an excellent place to begin is in antifeminist works of both women and men that ground their critique of women's behavior in the supposedly natural female body.

> As long as the bodily constitution of the species
> shall remain the same . . .
>
> —Lucy Aikin

Female and male writers on the condition of women, regardless of their ideological commitments, never failed to address women's corporeal state and the dangers or potential they saw grounded in women's bodies. As with the Romantic era's debate over women's reason and rights, which so much scholarly work has already addressed, the debate on women's bodies and bodily limitations also spanned a continuum of political interests and agendas. Mary Wollstonecraft's work embodies the entire range of approaches to the female body and the call for its reformation, as we will soon discover; she argued for greater physical strength both in the interests of domestic motherhood (strength as domestic forbearance, and necessary for raising healthy citizens) and in the interests of revolutionary feminism (strength as the final barrier of inequality holding women back from full participation in the public sphere and its rights).

This range of approaches to women's corporeal potential also includes more conservative and nonradical feminist writers such as Hannah More, Maria Edgeworth, Lucy Aikin, Priscilla Wakefield, and the conservative male writers on women such as Thomas

Gisborne, Thomas Taylor, and Richard Polwhele. These writers share a commitment to class status quo and urge women's increased physical hardiness in terms of their duties as mothers and/or laborers. For example, the Quaker feminist Priscilla Wakefield, in *Reflections on the Present Condition of the Female Sex* (1798) argued that "there is no reason for maintaining any sexual distinctions in the bodily exercises of children; if it is right to give both sexes all the corporal advantages, which nature has formed them to enjoy, let them both partake of the same rational means of obtaining a flow of health and animal spirits, to enable them to perform the stations of life."[16] However, Wakefield is concerned with how women can best perform the duties in each of the four classes (noble, wealthy, middle class, and laboring poor), and thus does not advocate a revolution, though she does want increased access for women to traditionally male professions. She also advocates dress reform, but debates the use of leather bodices and whalebone stays in terms of their effects on women's labor productivity: "far from these unyielding machines affording support to the wearer, and assisting her to perform laborious employments with greater ease, they are a painful impediment to the motions of the body, and prevent the full exertion of her strength" (*R*, 26).[17] Thus, like Wollstonecraft's earlier, more conservative, works (*Education of Daughters, Original Stories*), these works on the woman question emphasize the physical requirements of women's domestic duties, yet their consistent focus on the female body and its construction (as maternal) indicates that writers of this time were consciously aware that the "natural" features and abilities of the female body were vulnerable to fierce contestation.

Lucy Aikin, Anna Laetitia Barbauld's niece, was known primarily for her historical works and her children's literature. Like Robinson and Wollstonecraft, Aikin explicitly identified women's physical inferiority as the basis of men's ability to enforce their domination. But both Wollstonecraft and Aikin, despite their political differences, put this natural immutability of bodily constitution in conditional terms—"as long as," "if it is true that," "it seems that"—thus inviting the (at least speculative) possibility that this problem of unequal constitution has a history—that it will not always exist, or that it has not always existed. Aikin, like her more radical feminist contemporaries, also grounds her (more limited) claim for women's rights in the discourse of spiritual equality through reason. In *Epistles on Women* (1810), she rejects Pope's and Milton's "blasphemous presumptions" that women's intellect is nonexistent, and believes that men's dominion over

women is grounded in their ability to physically harm others.[18]
Men's power over women, however, is "no tyranny, being founded
not on an usurpation, but on certain unalterable necessities" (*EW*,
v). Aikin does not advocate changing this "unalterable" state of
women's oppression as Robinson does, though she may put it in
conditional terms:

> *As long as the bodily constitution of the species shall remain the same*, man
> must in general assume those public and active offices in life which
> confer authority, whilst to woman will usually be allotted such domes-
> tic and private ones as imply a certain degree of subordination.
>   Nothing therefore could, in my opinion, be more foolish than the
> attempt to engage our sex in a struggle for stations that they are
> physically unable properly to fill; for power of which they must always
> want the means to possess themselves. (*EW*, v–vi, emphasis added)

Though she begins her introduction by renouncing "entirely the
absurd idea that the two sexes ever can be, or ever ought to be,
placed in all respects on a footing of equality" (*EW*, v), Aikin also
reflects on the change which brought about women's inferiority
by rewriting Milton's account of Adam and Eve: "Alike the children of no partial God; / *Equal* they trod till want and guilt arose, /
Till savage blood was spilt, and man had foes" (*EW*, 12). Aikin thus
writes of a prelapsarian equality in which violence and physical
strength, not women's moral weakness, brought about the fall into
difference and tyranny.
    The descent into (male) violence marks the irreversible descent
into difference for Aikin. Perhaps then we could say that the
descent into *female* violence marks the end of difference. The
mutability of the female body into monstrous, unfemininely large,
and violent possibilities marks women's indifference to men's
natural dominion. Though Aikin did not leave such a possibility
open, she shares with Robinson, and, as we shall see, with Wollstonecraft, an awareness that the sexed body is a key site for political struggle. Aikin believes that the struggle is lost before even
attempted: "Nothing therefore could . . . be more foolish than
the attempt to engage our sex in a struggle for stations that they
are physically unable to properly fill" (*EW*, vi). But not all women,
or men, dismissed women's struggle to transgress or transform
the boundaries of their sexed body and subjectivity. Women's violence and the physical mutability it signals are part of a larger
tradition of resistance to Enlightenment taxonomy and bourgeois
class and gender differentiation. Terry Castle has argued convinc-

ingly that throughout the eighteenth century, masquerade, carnival, and travesty created a subversive "culture of travesty" in which the oppositional differences on which Enlightenment ideology depended were destabilized, and anomalous, monstrous, or phantastic bodies were temporarily celebrated: "it was the very fluidity of carnival—the way it subverted the dualities of male and female, animal and human, dark and light, life and death—that made it so inimical to the new 'atomizing' sensibility that heralded the development of modern bourgeois society."[19]

And of course not only women violated the Enlightenment's normalizing categories—the Chevalier/e d'Eon's celebrated, decades-long performance as a man pretending to be a woman who dressed as a man destabilized sexual dimorphism by foregrounding the "fluid, mutable, and elastic" distinctions among sexed bodies; as historian Gary Kates persuasively argues,

> D'Eon was then neither a transvestite, nor a transsexual, nor for that matter was he a "homosexual" anymore than he was a "heterosexual," or even a "man" nor "woman." The fact is that contemporary theorists of gender identity cannot help us understand d'Eon because d'Eon does not fit into any of the categories used by modern psychology.[20]

The physically aggressive women in Robinson's essay and Wollstonecraft's works are similarly at odds with traditional binary models of gender and sex. For a woman to be "unsexed," as was Wollstonecraft herself in conservative eyes (i.e., a "hyaena in petticoats" according to Horace Walpole), is not the same as becoming male. As I have argued elsewhere,[21] the unsexed female is *unfemale*, a third term in an anomalous position outside the two-sex binary, that, like the Chevalier/e d'Eon, attests to the limitations of modern sexual dimorphism. Modern feminist rejections of such unsexed females as simply masculine, merely inverting patriarchal gender polarity, attest to the limitations dimorphism and identity politics place on liberal feminism in particular.[22] But because these women writers lived in a time when sexual dimorphism was still in competition with an older one-sex model, as Thomas Laqueur has demonstrated in *Making Sex,* we need to revise our models in order to engage these writers productively. Their placement of biological sexual difference in conditional, historical terms would otherwise continue to remain below our threshold of interest, and thus we would fail to recognize these early origins of a feminist critique of the sexed body.

> I find that strength of mind has, in most cases,
> been accompanied by strength of body.
> —Mary Wollstonecraft

Mary Wollstonecraft's "deep ambivalence about sexuality"[23] in *Vindication of the Rights of Woman* has become an accepted and much lamented fact, argued for most eloquently by Cora Kaplan and Mary Poovey. Such a reading of Wollstonecraft's strategic repression of women's passions, however, threatens to conflate sexuality with corporeality. This reduction of the corporeal to its sexual dimensions makes possible the exaggerated further assertion that Wollstonecraft offered women a disembodied subjectivity, and that on the female body she offered only warnings against the passions, setting up nineteenth-century feminism's "heartbreaking conditions for women's liberation—a little death, the death of desire, the death of female pleasure" ("WN," 39). While I share Kaplan's and Poovey's observation that Wollstonecraft suspected "that female [sexual] appetite might be the precipitating cause of women's cultural objectification,"[24] I do not believe we can say, as Poovey does, that this distrust of sexuality "helps account for her vehement disgust with female physicality" (*PL,* 76) in general. Wollstonecraft, like Mary Robinson, offered women much more on the subject of the body than warnings about the need to suppress it in order for women to gain access to equal political rights as rational citizens.

Throughout *Rights of Woman,* Wollstonecraft links physical strength with mental strength, and repeatedly urges women to pursue both. In her critiques of soldiers and coquettes, she also connects her critique of each group's character (and of the ideology they embody) to the state of their bodies and the way their bodies are acculturated and disciplined. In fact, Wollstonecraft's sensitivity to the impact of bodily discipline on subjectivity has been pointed out by Susan Bordo as an example of a proto-Foucauldian feminist history of the (gendered) body:

> neither Foucault nor any other poststructuralist thinker discovered nor invented the "seminal" idea . . . that the "definition and shaping" of the body is "the focal point for struggles over the shape of power." *That* was discovered by feminism, and long before it entered into its recent marriage with poststructuralist thought—as far back, indeed, as Mary Wollstonecraft's 1792 description of the production of the "docile body" of the domesticated woman of privilege.[25]

Wollstonecraft, drawing on Macaulay, went further than observing how women's characters (their minds) are disciplined and formed through the body, however. She urged women to resist actively this normalization by altering their bodies, thus leaving open the possibility that physical sexual difference (as well as gender) is not natural but constructed and therefore can be shaped.

Wollstonecraft's pronouncement that "it is time to effect a revolution in female manners"[26] is implicitly grounded in a revolution in female corporeal normalization and discipline. Thus her suggestion that we "make [women] . . . , as part of the human species, labour by reforming themselves to reform the world" (*VRW*, 45) should be taken literally as well as figuratively—women can and must literally re-form themselves, physically and mentally, for "dependence of body naturally produces dependence of mind" (*VRW*, 43).

The risk in thus engaging Wollstonecraft's project of reform on both mental and physical grounds is that of exacerbating the mind/body binary split by yet again highlighting it. Yet feminism's historical struggle to undermine this binary opposition, as well as all such binaries, was central to eighteenth-century feminism's self-conscious resistance against the Enlightenment's explicit gendering of reason (masculine) and the passions (feminine). Thus Wollstonecraft's repeated calls to strengthen the mind *and* body, and my own attention to these instances, represent more than a capitulation to masculinist binary categories. Wollstonecraft and Robinson destabilized these two distinct categories, mind and body, not only by insisting on women's mental equality to men, thus resisting the Enlightenment's masculinization of reason, but also by focusing on the connections between mind and body as they relate to women's oppression. Their resistance to the ideology of incommensurable difference suggests a possibility for physical equality as an additional means for gaining political equality, while grounding political and philosophical critique of female oppression in the body.

By urging women to re-form themselves on two levels, physical and mental, Wollstonecraft is going beyond her period's increasingly aggressive demand that women's political agency be limited to the private domain, to the cultivation of a feminine self. According to this new ideology of domestic femininity or "republican motherhood," which in many ways Wollstonecraft articulated,[27] women's political agency, their power of social reform, is localized and personalized in their identities as mothers and educators of future public citizens, their sons. Poovey in fact isolates Wollstonecraft's tendency to revolutionize solely women's private characters, instead of their public roles, as one of her project's greatest short-comings: "Women are simply to wait for this revolution to *be* effected, for their dignity to *be* restored, for their reformation to *be* made necessary. The task is primarily men's, and it involves not confrontation but self-control" (*PL,* 79). Women's subjectivity, even for Wollstonecraft, is then synonymous with their subjection to a regime of self-regulation, according to this ideology of domestic femininity which successfully established cultural hegemony during the late eighteenth century. And yet Wollstonecraft's interest in corporeal reform exceeds this purpose of self-regulation and normalization, even while it relies on the mind/body split that makes this ideology of women's disembodied and depoliticized subjectivity possible.

> From the constitution of their bodies, men seem to be
> designed by Providence to attain a greater degree of virtue.
> —Mary Wollstonecraft

The key to grasping Wollstonecraft's subtle evocations of a re-formed female body lies in her much-acclaimed "double-voiced" discourse in the *Vindication of the Rights of Woman.* Gary Kelly's powerful argument in *Revolutionary Feminism: The Mind and Career of Mary Wollstonecraft* credits Wollstonecraft with creating a "revolution in discourse" in order to articulate women's interests in the late eighteenth-century middle-class cultural revolution: Wollstonecraft's "argument has elements of rational, general, abstract and 'philosophical' method, but is formulated in terms of 'women's sphere' of common, quotidian, domestic life, and expressed in what would be seen by many readers as a 'woman's voice.'"[28] Because Wollstonecraft uses what Kelly terms "feminine" discourses (conduct books, romances, familiar letters) and "masculine" discourses (philosophical treatises, polemics), I would argue that her usage of certain key terms, most notably *strength* and *virtue,* confounds the gender difference upon which the terms normally rely and leaves open a possibility for women to take on masculine physical and mental characteristics. Using both masculine and feminine notions of strength and virtue, simultaneously and ambiguously, Wollstonecraft can claim to leave certain "natural" distinctions in place (such as men's superior strength), even while her language works against such natural distinctions by describing women with the same "masculine" terms.

Central to Wollstonecraft's *Rights of Woman* is a debate on the nature of strength and weakness:

> I wish to persuade women to endeavour to acquire strength, both of mind and body, and to convince them that the soft phrases, susceptibility of heart, delicacy of sentiment, and refinement of taste, are almost synonymous with epithets of weakness. (*VRW*, 9)

Wollstonecraft repudiates traditional *ancien régime* femininity as an unnatural effect of women's oppression; weakness of body and mind has been constructed and should be reconstructed, she argues throughout. We are accustomed to focusing on her "strength" as mental or moral—yet what does she mean by physical strength? The strength to regulate the passions? The strength to endure injury and abuse? The strength to remain impregnable under attack? The strength to labor in any profession? The strength to retaliate, attack or kill? The strength to grow larger?

Clearly these different senses of strength are gendered; self-regulation was by this time almost exclusively associated with women;[29] strength as impregnability or resistance against pain also are important qualities of the domestic woman. Strength as the ability to perform physical labor is best understood in terms of its function to distinguish the classes; strength belonged to laboring women as a sign of their inferior refinement and proximity to a state of "barbarism,"[30] and to men in general due to their masculinity (part of the circular argument of natural difference). Strength as the ability to grow larger is characteristically masculine, since women were praised for diminutive stature during this time, and monstrous women were typically monstrous because "abnormally" large.[31] Aggression also remained a quality of masculine strength through its link to virility. And the gender conflict within "strength" also arises in the word "virtue," because the realm of virtue, for so long a masculine domain of virility and courage through the etymological root *vir* [man], had become by this time domestic womanhood's quintessentially feminine personal and social mission, identical with sexual purity. Throughout Wollstonecraft's *Rights of Woman*, "strength" and "weakness" oscillate between these long-standing masculine and feminine connotations so that a curious subtext of women's possible physical reformation emerges. Because strength refers simultaneously to masculine force and feminine forbearance, the term endows strong women with an ambiguity extending to their biology.

"In the government of the physical world," writes Wollstonecraft in her introduction,

> it is observable that the female in point of strength is, in general,
> inferior to the male. This is the law of nature; and it does not appear
> to be suspended or abrogated in favour of woman. A degree of physi-
> cal superiority cannot, therefore, be denied. (*VRW*, 8)

She thus first establishes strength as a physical and masculine
quality, governed by immutable laws in favor of men. Yet in her
next treatment of strength, which I quoted earlier, when she calls
on women to "acquire strength, both of mind and body" (*VRW*,
9), this use of strength overlaps with feminine ones of forbearance
and self-control, for this strength is contrasted with the "weakness" in behavior, sentiment, and taste which women resort to in
order to gain men's pity and love.

In the section of *Original Stories from Real Life* (1788) titled "The
Benefit of Bodily Pain: Fortitude the Basis of Virtue," Wollstonecraft, quoting Rousseau, likewise collapsed physical strength into
the stoic, and in her context, feminine, virtue of forbearance:
"'The term virtue, comes from a word signifying strength. Fortitude of mind is, therefore, the basis of every virtue, and virtue
belongs to a being, that is weak in its nature, and strong only in
will and resolution.'"[32] The (female) body's strength is, in other
words, the strength of the mind to control the body. Wollstonecraft erases the androcentric origin of virtue in order to apply it
to women, and in so doing she duplicates the historical gender
shift "virtue" underwent. Yet this earlier, more conservative, usage
is contrasted with many instances in the *Rights of Woman* when
women's physical passivity (forbearance) in the face of male injustice is challenged: "A frail being should labour to be gentle. But
when forbearance confounds right and wrong, it ceases to be a
virtue" (*VRW*, 34). Thus for Wollstonecraft the issue of self-
defense becomes, as it did even more dramatically for Robinson,
the threshold where women cross over into physically active beings, where passive feminine "virtue" is destabilized by virtue's
older, masculine associations.

Following her concession in the introduction to the *Rights of
Woman* that a "law of nature" renders women inferior to men
in physical strength, she continues to make this concession, yet,
curiously, in conditional terms. But it is not clear why such condi-
tionals should be necessary if a natural law were in operation—
"acknowledging the inferiority of woman, according to the pres-

ent *appearance* of things" (*VRW*, 35), "their *apparent* inferiority with respect to bodily strength" (*VRW*, 11), "bodily strength *seems* to give man a natural superiority over woman" (*VRW*, 39; my emphases). Wollstonecraft places the natural law of male superior strength in conditional terms precisely because she knows it is not natural. Like so many of the other rhetorical concessions in the *Rights of Woman*, physical incommensurability is an assurance to her readers that her argument for women's advancement has limits.

I am not implying that Wollstonecraft possessed a postmodern understanding of the construction of the natural body; yet her advocacy of a disembodied (because desexualized) feminism has been overstated, especially since her contemporary critics objected to the apparently limitless potential for female physical reform that they saw in her works. As she herself regularly paired corporeal and mental strength, so did Richard Polwhele and Thomas Taylor in their critiques of *Rights of Woman*. In *The Unsex'd Females* (1798), Polwhele is particularly disturbed by Wollstonecraft's call for women to violate the laws of nature by increasing their strength and abandoning their empire of beauty. Wollstonecraft, says Polwhele, calls on women to discard "each little artifice . . . , / No more by weakness winning fond regard" and to "nobly boast the firm gymnastic nerve." He clarifies this last statement with a footnote: "Miss Wollstonecraft seriously laments the neglect of all muscular exercises, at our female Boarding-schools." The list of "unsex'd women" who answer Wollstonecraft's call in the poem are compared to Spartan women trained for military battle, since they engage in "corporeal struggles mix'd with mental strife."[33]

Thomas Taylor also foregrounds Wollstonecraft's ideas on altering women's corporeal abilities in his parody of *Rights of Woman* titled *A Vindication of the Rights of Brutes* (1792).[34] Taylor ridicules Wollstonecraft's and Paine's critique of gender and class distinctions, respectively, by extending their arguments of equality to nonhuman animals, an idea he trusts readers will find absurd. According to Taylor, Wollstonecraft's call for women's equality, like his for the equality of all animals, "will perhaps appear to many too abstracted and refined, and as having a tendency to destroy those distinctions of society, which seem to have been pointed out by nature herself" (*VRB*, 14). Yet he of course proceeds to destroy such "natural distinctions" between human and nonhuman animals, citing Wollstonecraft's assertion of equality in physical strength as his (presumably absurd) precedent:

> this sublime doctrine [of universal equality] is daily gaining ground amongst the thinking part of mankind . . . . Mrs. Woolstoncraft [*sic*]

has indisputably proved, that women are in every respect naturally equal to men, not only in mental abilities, but likewise in bodily strength, *boldness,* and the like. (*VRB,* 10–11)

Of course, Wollstonecraft had not argued that women are equal in bodily strength to men, but had, as I have shown, called for increased female strength while conceding a natural (and conditional) male superiority, the rhetorical nature of which seems to have been clear to Taylor and Polwhele.[35]

Wollstonecraft's assurance of "naturally" superior male strength is not only placed in conditional terms, but as her critics realized, leaves open the disturbing possibility that women may continue to push the limits of corporeal distinctions to such a degree that the sexual order itself would be threatened on its supposedly most incontestable ground, that of natural corporeal difference. For when she assures her audience that "men have superior strength of body," she immediately proposes:

Let us then, by being allowed to take the same exercise as boys, not only during infancy, but youth, arrive at perfection of body, that we may know how far the natural superiority of man extends. (*VRW,* 85)

For all her assurances to the contrary, then, Wollstonecraft does leave open the possibility of an ever receding limit to women's corporeal strength, and thus an eventual end to men's "natural superiority." This stance is similar to Godwin's on physical perfectibility in *Enquiry Concerning Political Justice,* yet readings of Godwin (as of Wollstonecraft) have traditionally emphasized the idealism and aversion to physicality in his concept of the mind which can transform and even eliminate the limits and desires of the body.[36] Despite her own belief in human moral perfectibility, influenced by Richard Price's ideas, this charge of disembodied perfectibility cannot be leveled at Wollstonecraft unless one reduces her argument on women's bodies to a warning on the dangers of sexual passion (a warning which she most assuredly did give). Even when she wrote of women's minds, she consistently employed the physical metaphor of size, urging women to "strengthen the female mind by enlarging it" (*VRW,* 24), thus drawing together mind and body in a physically grounded philosophy that called for an end to the limits on the size and strength of women.

Wollstonecraft, in arguing that "genteel women are, literally speaking, slaves to their bodies, and glory in their subjection"

(*VRW*, 43–44) is far from anticipating Foucault's famous reversal in *Discipline and Punish* that the soul is the prison of the body. Wollstonecraft's enlightenment discourse of liberty still relies on a negative model of power, precisely the model overturned by Foucault in his model of power as productive and normalizing even as it is repressive. Yet what is most important is that Wollstonecraft and other feminists of her time had a clear sense that the female body is an ideological construct, and that they urged women to adopt exercises, sexual behavior, adornment, and diet[37] that would offer them increased political and intellectual opportunities. These feminists returned to the issue of corporeal practice and construction, going against the grain of their reliance on immutable "natural" characteristics such as sympathy, reason, or benevolence with which we are more familiar.

The Beginning and the End of Difference

Modern feminist theory has done much to problematize and historicize the construction of the female body, especially as it relates to weight management, reproduction, sexuality, and disease. Physical strength remains associated with masculinity, however, and calling for women to become stronger, as Wollstonecraft and Robinson do, is dismissed by some as an end to femaleness and an absorption of the female body by the male universal, sometimes disguised as the androgynous body. One might argue that my reading of strong bodies reinscribes a masculinist model of strength and power in which autonomous, stable subjects and bodies possess power over others, a model of power overturned by both Foucault and feminism. Could these early feminists' interest in strong bodies simply be dismissed as an unfortunate result of their acceptance of the (masculine) gendering of power, and of women's exclusion from "power" in the domestic sphere? Foucauldian feminist studies of this period, such as Nancy Armstrong's *Desire and Domestic Fiction*, focus on precisely the domestic sphere of power that has historically been defined as disempowered, silent, and exiled, and reveal the class interests which bourgeois domestic women articulated and benefited from as part of this private sphere. A Foucauldian model of power exercised through technologies of the self, then, has proven invaluable to feminist critiques of what constitutes women's power and influence. And yet these feminist revisions of power do not exclude the possibilities of power in strength, nor the reduction of strength to masculinity; rather, it is these associations (of strength with masculinity) themselves which have been the objects of Foucauldian and feminist scrutiny, and should not therefore be passed over as transhistorically stable and stabilizing.

Wollstonecraft and other feminists did maintain an interest in a negative model of power, in which the autonomous, stable self must conform to external power while exercising a similar control over its internal hierarchy of sentiment and appetites. Yet her interest in women's increasing physical strength, activity, and size is much more than a rejection of femaleness as the price for becoming fully enfranchised citizens with "masculinized" selves and bodies. Wollstonecraft found feminist potential in stronger and larger bodies because they could transform the very ground of the sex/gender system. The strong female body transforms gender, which early feminists such as Wollstonecraft, Robinson, and Macaulay knew to be culturally constructed, by transforming "natural" sexual difference itself, which they suspected could be altered. Physical strength was central to these women's conception of the political order and men's dominion in it; thus despite their simultaneous interest in women's cultural power as republican mothers, they pursued inquiries into women's cultural and political power through manipulating and controlling hierarchical biological difference, the possibility of which threatened their cultural authority as republican mothers. Thus even in the beginnings of modern Western feminism do we find the end of difference, the identity crisis modern feminism is confronting anew.

But is this interest in minimizing biological difference by increasing strength and size the end of "femaleness"? Certainly in late twentieth-century Western culture the idealization of women's slenderness and youth amounts to a normalizing standard best met by the preadolescent male body. Susan Bordo persuasively argues against the subversive effects of the "empowering" images of strong, self-disciplined, slim bodies, as used in advertising, in *Unbearable Weight: Feminism, Western Culture and the Body.* Thus in this modern Western context, the influence of the diet and fitness industries and mass media on the production of women's desires for strong and "healthy" bodies would problematize any resistance such "strength" would provide. But in the late eighteenth century, representations of women's physical strength were not yet a means of normalization, and were not co-opted by industries through advertising. Pat Rogers has traced the beginning of weight management to this period, however, and specifically to the novel, arguing that the body, both male and female, as natural given began to be replaced by a notion of the body as malleable.[38] The connection between weight management and strong bodies lies in this concept of mutability and of the body as site and agent of cultural production. Women's own representations of the mutable female body cannot be dismissed as misogynist depictions of the dangerous animality or disease-prone instability of women's bodies; these representations are examples of women's own contributions to the prevailing medical and political models of sex and gender which they are too often assumed simply to have received (from masculinist power) and either absorbed or rejected. We cannot afford to ignore these early feminists' own doubts as to the naturalness, and even the value, of "femaleness" as distinct corporeal difference.

Wollstonecraft, Robinson, Macaulay, Aikin, all suggested that an inequality in power (political, intellectual, economic, and/or physical) predated and constituted corporeal difference, understood in the limited aspect of a gendered inequality of physical strength. The question of the nature of the relationship between power, sex, and gender is thus simply moved back in time and still unanswered, for the nature of the "original" power that allowed men to enforce political domination of women through physical violence, and enabled the construction of "the weaker sex," is placed in a prehistorical and prelapsarian void by Wollstonecraft, Robinson, and even Aikin. And it is not clear that "man" and "woman" existed before this power imbalance. We can understand this gesture of placing sexual indifference "outside" history as an utopian one, parallel to the nostalgia for the precultural, prepatriarchal feminine, and one that has remained a part of certain feminisms to this day. But it is not as such a nostalgic gesture that I wish to examine women's visions of undifferentiated or mutable bodies, for as Butler has argued:

> The postulation of the "before" within feminist theory becomes politically problematic when it constrains the future to materialize an idealized notion of the past or when it supports . . . the reification of a precultural sphere of the authentic feminine. (*GT*, 36)

One could read these women's speculations on the origins of sexual differentiation, and the possibility of a lost precultural and prelapsarian sexual equality, as part of a larger Romantic project of imagining and pursuing a unified, authentic and androgynous body and self. The androgynous bodies and selves dreamed of by

Percy Bysshe Shelley and Blake, for example, are typically read as an eclipse of the feminine by the masculine universal in its quest for self-sufficient totality.[39] Yet the concept of androgyny as lost authenticity, while accurate for Shelley and Blake, is not precisely what these women's representations of increased strength suggest. As Wollstonecraft described her relationship to Rousseau, it is he who looks for lost authenticities, while she seeks them in the future: "Rousseau exerts himself to prove that all *was* right originally: a crowd of authors that all *is* now right: and I, that all will *be* right" (*VRW*, 15).

Masculinization and sexlessness, rather than idealized lost androgyny, were the terms in which Wollstonecraft considered the future transformation of sex and gender. Wollstonecraft specifically denounced women who were masculinized in a certain respect—in taking up violent sports, and by extension all violent activity, as her demonization of the October Days marchers shows. She clearly did not want women to replicate a system of violence by becoming agents of that violence; yet this rejection of violence is, of course, also a rhetorical strategy: "because I am a woman, I would not lead my readers to suppose that I mean violently to agitate the contested question respecting the equality of inferiority of the sex" (*VRW*, 8). What is most interesting is that Wollstonecraft's feminism allowed for the possibility of a continuum of biological difference despite a simultaneous belief in binary sexual difference. More recently, in *Equivocal Beings*, Claudia Johnson has also argued that for Wollstonecraft "manliness and liberty are virtually synonymous" (*EB*, 31), and has demonstrated the extent of Wollstonecraft's anxiety over men's and women's growing physical and mental effeminacy:

> *Rights of Woman* is premised on the possibility that the virtue of manliness is accessible to female as well as to male minds and bodies, but the evidence seems to be that if sex can be separated from gender in women's case, it can in men's as well, and that the "natural" masculinity she is idealizing may only be a construction too. (*EB*, 45)

But I think we can and should go further; I think Wollstonecraft fully realized that this natural "manliness," which I have termed *strength*, was in fact a construction, and that she saw strength as a quality that both established and destabilized boundaries between sex and class, making it both dangerous and potentially revolutionary, and thus absolutely central to her project.

Wollstonecraft's emphasis on women's revolution and re-formation, and her belief in human moral perfectibility, contrib-uted to her suspicion that sexed bodies have changed and will continue to change, and that in her historical context, it was im-perative that women, increasingly defined by their "weakness," struggle to grow stronger and to enlarge their mental and physi-cal faculties. Her concept of the "sexless" mind and soul, like that of the strong body, is thus not parallel to male Romantics' ori-ginary androgyny and its cannibalization of the phantasmatic (fe-male) Other.

> Active evil is better than passive good.
>   —William Blake

Wollstonecraft's conception of sex and gender connects her not to Romantic androgyny but to Sade's concept of social hierarchy where power and not sex is the ordering principle. During the Reign of Terror, Wollstonecraft wrote in "A Letter on the Charac-ter of the French Nation" that she had lost the "perspective of the golden age" where benevolence and reason are the order of the day;

> and, losing thus in part my theory of a more perfect state, start not, my friend, if I bring forward an opinion, which at the first glance seems to be levelled against the existence of God! I am not become an Atheist, I assure you, by residing at Paris: yet I begin to fear that vice, or, if you will, evil, is the prime mobile of action, and that, when the passions are justly poized, we become harmless, and in the same proportion useless.[40]

If we connect Wollstonecraft's confession that she fears evil is the prime mover of action to her much-criticized call for revolution that does not advocate for women's agitation and public activism, we can infer the cost she is not willing to pay for women's revolu-tion—women's violence. The women who marched on Versailles were demonized by Wollstonecraft (and conservative writers) be-cause their violence and mobilization signified a corporeal disrup-tion, a violation of the system of sexual dimorphism:

> a multitude of women by some impulse were collected together. . . . The concourse, at first, consisted mostly of market women, and the lowest refuse of the streets, women who had thrown off the virtues

of one sex without having power to assume more than the vices of the other.[41]

Wollstonecraft depicts the bodies of these violent women as the grotesque body of the crowd, characterized by a lack of proper boundaries between sexes and classes, and most importantly by a lack of unified purpose, since they were gathered "by some impulse": "such a rabble has seldom been gathered together; and they quickly showed, that their movement was not the effect of public spirit" (*FR*, 197).

Wollstonecraft's emphasis on the unpredictable and radical mobility of this body of women is most significant for my discussion. It is the women's emotional and physical violence, or in Wollstonecraft's terms, "evil," that effects radical political change. As these women assume a public, militant position, their distinct bodies degenerate and they throw off their feminine subjectivity (the virtues of their sex). It is precisely such a violent sexual revolution that Wollstonecraft's texts momentarily consider and push to the margins; for the price of this revolution, the dissolution of the proper (middle-class) female body and its virtues, is simply too high for (middle-class) women to pay, as Wollstonecraft saw it.

Yet such a concept of mobility and change driven by destruction and not creation finds an interesting parallel in Sade, and one which helps us better understand the radical potential of violence against difference in Wollstonecraft's time at which she hinted but from which she drew back. For Wollstonecraft's fear that "evil" drives the universe was precisely Sade's point, and one which he celebrated with unequaled ferocity in all his works. In *Philosophy in the Bedroom*, Sade wrote:

> The primary and most beautiful of Nature's qualities is motion, which agitates her at all times, but this motion is simply a perpetual consequence of crimes, she conserves it by means of crimes only; the person who most nearly resembles her, and therefore the most perfect being, necessarily will be the one whose most active agitation will become the cause of many crimes; whereas . . . the inactive or indolent person . . . the virtuous person, must be in her eyes . . . the least perfect.[42]

Sade's female libertines, most notably Juliette, like the "lowest refuse of the street" which Wollstonecraft had condemned, proliferate agitation and crime through their exuberant actions. This criminal motion and agitation lead not only to social disorder, as in the case of the women's march on Versailles, but to sexual disorder, as these agents of crime throw off their sex and assume that of a monstrous body which transgresses the boundaries of the proper bourgeois body. Sade's female libertines, like Wollstonecraft's marketwomen, also disturb the boundaries of a two-sex system through their agitation, possessing phallic clitorides while engaging in sexual acts that degenitalize the body, drawing pleasure from indiscriminate objects and bodily sites. These libertines still live in a two-class system, but the classes are strong and weak, or master and slave, and women, though largely in the weak class, can move into the class of masters by perpetrating crimes and causing the suffering of others. Sade's system of master and slave classes has been the focus of much feminist debate, and some (such as Simone de Beauvoir, Alice Laborde, and Angela Carter) argue that his model of power, because it unmasks the violence that underlies all sexual and social relations, serves the interests of feminism, especially since (admittedly exceptional) women like Juliette can move from one category to the other, something the two-sex system ostensibly disallows. Although Sade's female libertines are dismissed by other feminists as token women in masculinist institutions, it is clear on the other hand that, as Angela Carter argues, these token women are simultaneously "engaged in destroying those high places all the time that [they are] enjoying the pastimes they offer."[43] It is ultimately as agents of destruction (as opposed to traditionally feminine creation) that they are valuable to feminism.

In *Literature and Evil,* Bataille linked Sade's appreciation of destruction and radical disorder to Blake's Romantic celebration of transgressive energy (embodied in his proverb of hell, "Exuberance is beauty"). Wollstonecraft and Robinson also acknowledge the connection between radical political transformation and violence, specifically in the case of women, but ultimately could not advocate a sexual revolution based on this connection because it would mean the overthrow of woman's virtues as well as of her chains. Thus Wollstonecraft abandoned her original project on the French Revolution after reaching the disturbing conclusion during the Terror that "evil is the prime mobile of action," and instead began her *An Historical and Moral View of the Origin and Progress of the French Revolution,* which limits itself to the early, less problematic years of the revolution, although it was written during the Terror. Wollstonecraft's telling omission of the violence that surrounded her and her text affirms the dangerous centrality of that violence, specifically women's violence, to feminism's landmark texts and authors. For Wollstonecraft's negative account of the marketwomen's march on Versailles, which I quoted earlier, depends on a speculation, shared with conservative male writers, that women cannot move themselves to violent political action, but must be the unwitting dupes of conspiratorial (male) agitation:

> *That a body of women should put themselves in motion* to demand relief of the king, or to remonstrate with the assembly respecting the tardy manner of forming the constitution, *is scarcely probable;* and that they should have undertaken the business, without being instigated by designing persons, . . . is a belief which the most credulous will hardly swallow. (*FR*, 207, emphasis added)

In *The Cenci,* Percy Bysshe Shelley's Beatrice Cenci embodies his similar uncomfortable conclusion that all action implicates one in "evil" and cruelty, even if one is oneself a victim of cruelty; as Stuart Curran has argued: "Within the perverse framework of this tragedy, to act is to commit evil. The tragic premise admits of a second and less obvious reading: an evil act can only be met by another evil act. Good is by its nature fundamentally passive."[44] Beatrice's descent into evil is more disturbing than even Curran admits, I believe, for rather than representing "Everyman," Beatrice more precisely represents Everywoman, victim of sexual violence and injustice who responds with violence herself and confounds the difference between victim and aggressor. Women's action, such as Beatrice's or that of the Versailles mob, is implicated in active evil, which in turn threatens to destroy the very foundation of "natural" femininity, maternity and its life-affirming consolations. This demystification of the maternal body and its benevolence is, according to Angela Carter, the most dangerous price for women's emancipation, for "it represents the final secularization of mankind" (*SW*, 110).

Women's public violence thus threatened Wollstonecraft's revolutionary project as much as their private subjugation did, and her texts move to suppress this violence. Wollstonecraft's explanation of "moral progress" as the repression, not elimination, of public vice is a similar move to distance violence: "Are not . . . many of the vices, that formerly braved the face of day, now obliged to lurk, like beasts of prey, in concealment, till night allows them to roam at large" (*FR*, 110). The nature of these vices among the ancients is not specified, though previous examples of vices given are sadistic torture and killing by tyrants, as well as a reference to the Romans' "unnatural vices," probably referring to the public visibility and acceptance of certain forms of male homosexuality. This aversion to "unnatural [sexual] vices" may account for

Wollstonecraft's further enigmatic comments on moral progress: "And the odium which now forces several vices, that then passed as merely the play of the imagination, to hide their heads, may chase them out of society, when justice is common to all." The progress of moral justice thus requires the suppression of violence, and of transgressive "unnatural" sexualities—the public activities of marketwomen and of the queen are thus alike unacceptable because they make visible women's violence and sexuality, respectively.

The "beasts of prey" Wollstonecraft urges underground are those she witnessed during the Terror, and those which Sade and even Blake ushered into the open as agents of a destructive energy which, in Bataille's words, "incarnates revolutions." Women who incarnate revolution through physical violence are in the process of destroying the two-sex and two-gender system that gives them their identities as women, and provides us with the consolations of "natural" feminine nurturing and benevolence. Carter values Sade precisely because his "invention of Juliette is an emphatic denial of this entrancing rhetoric" of the sacredness of women (*SW*, 109). Feminism's crisis of identity has in fact always been with us, and the challenge that poststructuralism has posed to feminism's politics of identity began to emerge two hundred years ago, if we consider Sade in conjunction with Wollstonecraft, the father of poststructuralism and the mother of modern feminism.

Wollstonecraft's works hinted at a Sadeian world, one in which sex was more or less an effect of power, and in which women's revolutionary violence revealed not so much that women's nature is inherently violent, but that it is nonexistent, or rather that it is a necessary illusion. The consequences of women adopting such a Sadeian perspective were considered in more direct terms by Robinson:

> Supposing women were to act upon the same principle of egotism, consulting their own inclinations, interest, and amusement only, (and there is no law of Nature which forbids them; none of any species but that which is framed by man;) what would be the consequences? The annihilation of all moral and religious order. So that every good which cements the bonds of civilized society, originates wholly in the forbearance, and conscientiousness of woman. (*LWE*, 86–87)

Robinson was prepared to accept women's nature as a necessary illusion, necessary for nothing less than maintaining all moral and religious order. We too must be careful not to depend uncritically on the terms "woman" and "woman's text" as if they were transhistorically stable, without acknowledging that a "history of the novel [cannot] be historical if it fails to take into account the history of sexuality" (*DDF*, 10). Even politically conservative writers of the late eighteenth century feared that women's inferiority in strength, to which they ascribed men's ability to enforce their dominance, was a product of history and not of nature, and that "woman" herself, on the corporeal level, was, in Butler's words, "a term in process, a becoming, a constructing" (*GT*, 33). Though it may be disturbing at times, as Wollstonecraft's horrified reaction to the Parisian marketwomen demonstrates, we can no longer afford to ignore women's and feminism's active role, and undeniable interest, in destroying the very consolations of difference on which modern feminism is based.

Notes

1. I am grateful to Greg Clingham, Donna Landry, John Logan, Kari Lokke, and Mary Peace for their helpful comments on earlier drafts of this essay.

2. From *Discours aux mânes de Marat et Le Pelletier,* as quoted in Chantal Thomas, "Heroism in the Feminine: Charlotte Corday and Madame Roland," *The Eighteenth Century: Theory and Interpretation* 30 (1989): 74–75.

3. Germaine de Staël, "On Women Writers" (1800), in *An Extraordinary Woman: Selected Writings of Germaine de Staël,* trans. Vivian Folkenflik (New York: Columbia University Press, 1987), 201.

4. Lynn Hunt, "The Unstable Boundaries of the French Revolution," in *A History of Private Life.* Vol. 4: *From the Fires of the Revolution to the Great War,* ed. Michelle Perrot, trans. Arthur Goldhammer (Cambridge: Harvard University Press, 1990), 13, 45.

5. Madelyn Gutwirth, *The Twilight of the Goddesses: Women and Representation in the French Revolutionary Era* (New Brunswick: Rutgers University Press, 1992), 383.

6. Mary Robinson, *Monody to the Memory of the Late Queen of France* (London, 1793).

7. Joan Landes, *Women and the Public Sphere in the Age of the French Revolution* (Ithaca: Cornell University Press, 1988), 12.

8. Katharine Rogers, "The View from England," in *French Women and the Age of Enlightenment,* ed. Samia Spencer (Bloomington: Indiana University Press, 1984), 360–61.

9. Anne Frances Randall [Mary Robinson], *A Letter to the Women of England, on the Injustice of Mental Subordination. With Anecdotes* (London: Longman & Rees, 1799), 18. This text is reprinted in part in *Women in the Eighteenth Century: Constructions of Femininity,* ed. Vivien Jones (New York: Routledge, 1990). All citations, however, are from the 1799 text in the British Library; hereafter *LWE,* cited in the text.

10. Samuel Richardson, *Pamela: or, Virtue Rewarded* (New York: Norton, 1958), 214.

11. Robinson's example is based on the actual court case of Ann Broderick, who shot her lover in 1794, and was found not guilty by reason of insanity. The judge instructed the jury that while passion or jealousy were not sufficient grounds for declaring her insane, the fact that she laughed aloud after shooting him, "was a striking, and almost infallible symptom of insanity." See *The Trial of Miss Broderick, for the Wilful Murder of George Errington, Esq.* (Edinburgh: Robertson, 1795), 13.

CRACIUN: VIOLENCE AGAINST DIFFERENCE

12. At the conclusion of Robinson's example, the lady returns to the sentimental tradition from which she had strayed, retiring to a convent and dying from longing for her dead lover.

13. Mary Wollstonecraft, *A Vindication of the Rights of Men*, 2d ed. (London, 1790), in *Political Writings: Rights of Men, Rights of Woman, French Revolution*, ed. Janet Todd (Toronto: University of Toronto Press, 1993), 15.

14. Judith Butler, *Gender Trouble: Feminism and the Subversion of Identity* (New York: Routledge, 1992), 7; hereafter *GT*, cited in the text.

15. Chris Cullens, "Mrs. Robinson and the Masquerade of Womanliness," in *Body and Text in the Eighteenth Century*, ed. Veronica Kelly and Dorothea Von Mücke (Stanford: Stanford University Press, 1994), 267.

16. Priscilla Wakefield, *Reflections on the Present Condition of the Female Sex* (New York: Garland, 1974), 20; hereafter *R*, cited in the text.

17. Similarly, the anonymous author of *The Female Aegis, or, The Duties of Women from Childhood to Old Age* (London: Ginger, 1798) affirms the necessity of women being permitted to develop "a strong constitution" through exercise, inasmuch as this physical strength will "communicate to [the mind's] powers an accession of strength" and allow women to forbear with "steady spirits" and a "strong and alert mind" (31–32).

18. Lucy Aikin, *Epistles on Women, Exemplifying Their Character and Conditions in Various Ages and Nations* (London, 1810), vi. The first section of this poem is reprinted in *Nineteenth-Century Women's Poetry*, ed. Isobel Armstrong and Joseph Bristow (Oxford: Clarendon Press, 1996), 129–33; hereafter *EW*, cited in the text.

19. Terry Castle, *Masquerade and Civilization: The Carnivalesque in Eighteenth-Century Culture and Fiction* (Stanford: Stanford University Press, 1986), 103.

20. Gary Kates, "D'Eon Returns to France: Gender and Power in 1777," in *Body Guards: The Cultural Politics of Gender Ambiguity*, ed. Julia Epstein and Kristina Straub (New York: Routledge, 1991), 186. Wollstonecraft mentions d'Eon in the *Rights of Woman*, listing her as one of the exceptional women, along with Sappho and Macaulay, who transcend the limitations of their gender and therefore do not serve as models for average (middle-class) women (77). Robinson, in *Letter to the Women of England* used d'Eon as an example of the double standard applied to women's accomplishments, since when d'Eon "was discovered to be a WOMAN, the highest terms of praise were converted into, 'eccentricity, absurd and masculine temerity, at once ridiculous and disgusting'" (71).

21. Adriana Craciun, "'I hasten to be disembodied': Charlotte Dacre, the Demon Lover, and Representations of the Body," *European Romantic Review* 6 (1995): 75–97.

22. Scholars who maintain that travesty and transsexualism reinforce the patriarchal sexual binary include Janice Raymond in *The Transsexual Empire* (Boston: Beacon Press, 1979), Diane Dugaw in *The Woman Warrior and Popular Balladry, 1650–1850* (Cambridge: Cambridge University Press, 1989), and Catherine Craft-Fairchild in *Gender and Masquerade: Disguise and Female Identity in Eighteenth-Century Fictions by Women* (University Park: Pennsylvania State University Press, 1993). These critics share a reliance on a biological sexual dimorphism while calling for the separation of gender identity from such binary biological difference. Modern challenges to this belief in a stable and stabilizing sexual dimorphism include the work of Michel Foucault, Thomas Laqueur, Judith Butler, the volume *Third Sex, Third Gender: Beyond Sexual Dimorphism in Culture and History*, ed. Gilbert Herdt (New York: Zone Books, 1994), Arthur and Marilouise Kroker's anthology *The Last Sex: Feminism and Outlaw Bodies* (New York: St. Martin's Press, 1993), and even such nonacademic works as Kate Bornstein's *Gender Outlaw: On Men, Women, and the Rest of Us*.

23. Cora Kaplan, "Wild Nights: Pleasure/Sexuality/Feminism," in *Sea Changes: Essays on Culture and Feminism* (London: Verso, 1986), 41; hereafter "WN," cited in the text.

24. Mary Poovey, *The Proper Lady and the Woman Writer: Ideology as Style in the Works of Mary Wollstonecraft, Mary Shelley, and Jane Austen* (Chicago: University of Chicago Press, 1984), 76; hereafter *PL*, cited in the text.

25. See Susan Bordo, "Feminism, Foucault, and the Politics of the Body," in *Up against Foucault: Explorations of Some Tensions between Foucault and Feminism*, ed. Caroline Ramazanoglu (New York: Routledge, 1993), 185.

26. Mary Wollstonecraft, *Vindication of the Rights of Woman*, 2d ed., ed. Carol Poston (New York: Norton, 1975), 45; hereafter *VRW*, cited in the text.

27. We should, however, keep in mind Claudia Johnson's important point that "the centrality of maternity in Wollstonecraft's political thought has been exaggerated." See Johnson, *Equivocal Beings: Politics, Gender, and Sentimentality in the 1790s* (Chicago: University of Chicago Press, 1995), 215 n.3; hereafter *EB*, cited in the text.

28. Gary Kelly, *Revolutionary Feminism: The Mind and Career of Mary Wollstonecraft* (London: Macmillan, 1992), 108, 110.

29. Nancy Armstrong argues that in the eighteenth century conduct books shifted their focus from the aristocratic man to the middle-class woman, grounding the bourgeois ideology of self-transformation in the middle-class female body: "This transformational power still seems to arise from within the self and to affect that self through strategies of self-discipline, the most perfect realization of which is perhaps anorexia nervosa. What we encounter in books of instruction for women, then, is something on the order of Foucault's productive hypothesis that continues to work upon the material body unencumbered by political history because that body is the body of a woman." See Armstrong, *Desire and Domestic Fiction: A Political History of the Novel* (New York: Oxford University Press, 1987), 95; hereafter *DDF*, cited in the text.

30. See, for example, "Woman in an Uncultivated State" and "In Civilized Society" in *The Female Aegis*, 6–10

31. Examples include the female creature in *Frankenstein*, the Bleeding Nun in *The Monk*, Victoria in Charlotte Dacre's *Zofloya*, Vashti in Brontë's *Villette*, and Bertha in *Jane Eyre*. In *The Flesh Made Word* (New York: Oxford University Press, 1987), Helena Michie argues that by the early Victorian period thinness was a defining characteristic of the normal female body.

32. Wollstonecraft is quoting from Rousseau's *Émile; Original Stories from Real Life*, in *The Works of Mary Wollstonecraft*, ed. Janet Todd and Marilyn Butler, vol. 4 (London: Pickering, 1989), 437.

33. Richard Polwhele, *The Unsex'd Females* (New York: Garland, 1974), 14–15, 20–22.

34. Thomas Taylor, *A Vindication of the Rights of Brutes* (Gainesville: Scholars' Facsimiles and Reprints, 1966); hereafter *VRB*, cited in the text. Taylor (1758–1835), known as "The Platonist," was a friend of both Paine and Wollstonecraft, who had visited his house, though clearly he did not share their politics.

35. Robert Bisset in his novel *Modern Literature* (1804) similarly ridiculed Wollstonecraft's advocacy for women's increased physical activity; he complained that women "were to be coachmen postillions, blacksmiths, carpenters, coalheavers, &c . . . . She trusted the time would soon arrive when the sex would acquire high renown in boxing matches, sword and pistol" (as quoted in Johnson, *Equivocal Beings*, 11).

36. Catherine Gallagher argues this point persuasively in "The Body Versus the Social Body in the Works of Thomas Malthus and Henry Mayhew." See *The Making of the Modern Body: Sexuality and Society in the Nineteenth Century*, ed. Catherine Gallagher and Thomas Laqueur (Berkeley: University of California Press, 1987), 83–106.

37. Catharine Macaulay's belief, in *Letters on Education* (1790) (New York: Garland, 1974), that children not be brought up "to be devourers of animal substances" (38) is based on her understanding that the cruelty involved in consuming animal flesh perpetuates a

system of human oppression that denatures human sympathy: "It is a diet only fit for savages; and must naturally tend to weaken sympathy which Nature has given man, as the best guard against the abuse of the extensive power with which she has entrusted him" (39).

38. Pat Rogers, "Fat Is a Fictional Issue: The Novel and the Rise of Weight Watching," in *Literature and Medicine During the Eighteenth Century*, ed. W. F. Bynum and Roy Porter (New York: Routledge, 1993), 168–87.

39. For an overview of the misogyny implicit in the (male) phantasy of the androgyne, see Kari Weil, *Androgyny and the Denial of Difference* (Charlottesville: University Press of Virginia, 1992) and Diane Long Hoeveler, *Romantic Androgyny: The Woman Within* (University Park: Pennsylvania State University Press, 1990).

40. This letter, dated 15 February 1793, was intended to be the first in a series, but the project was abandoned, and the letter, whose full title is "Letter Introductory to a Series of Letters on the Present Character of the French Nation," was published in the first edition of Godwin's *Posthumous Works of the Author of "A Vindication of the Rights of Woman"* (1798); citations here are from *The Works of Mary Wollstonecraft*, ed. Janet Todd and Marilyn Butler, vol. 6 (London: Pickering, 1989), 444–45.

41. *An Historical and Moral View of the French Revolution*, in *The Works of Mary Wollstonecraft*, 6: 196–97; hereafter *FR*, cited in the text.

42. Marquis de Sade, *The Complete Justine, Philosophy in the Bedroom, and Other Writings*, trans. Richard Seaver and Austryn Wainhouse (New York: Grove Press, 1965), 520–21.

43. Angela Carter, *The Sadeian Woman and the Ideology of Pornography* (New York: Pantheon Books, 1978), 105–6; hereafter *SW*, cited in the text. The feminist debate on Sade is far-ranging, dynamic, and ongoing, and outside the scope of this paper. Briefly, feminists who are doubtful of Sade's usefulness to feminist projects include Nancy Miller, Andrea Dworkin, and Luce Irigaray.

44. Stuart Curran, "'The Cenci': The Tragic Resolution," *Percy Bysshe Shelley: Modern Critical Views*, ed. Harold Bloom (New York: Chelsea House, 1985), 75.

Forbidden Knowledge: Intertextual Discovery and Imitation in the French Revolution

Steven Blakemore
Florida Atlantic University

D URING the 1790s, the controversy over the French Revolution ballooned into a voluminous intertextual war in which a variety of texts were allusively invoked by the Revolution's supporters and opponents in a great Battle of Books evoking earlier intertextual wars over tradition and innovation. Supporters of the Revolution engaged in a radical critique of the conservative canon in an endeavor to replace it with a new revolutionary canon emphasizing epistemological light and discovery—liberation from the old confining canon of imitation and restraint. In England, the attack on the traditional canon was an attack on those texts that radicals believed reinforced the psychological slavery of people kept in ignorance and darkness—texts constituting the ideological authority of the Old Order. Radicals represented themselves rewriting the old terms through a rebellious reading of textual tradition—re-represented as imitative and derivative—reactionary "copies" of the oppressive ideological order. In contrast, they celebrated the new revolutionary knowledge that was liberating humanity, revealing new moral and political discoveries. But the terms of the new paradigms (knowledge, originality, discovery, and light) were a continuation of previous intertextual wars over tradition and iconoclasm, authority and innovation. In representing themselves as writing a new epistemological revolution, radicals were repeating old radical tradition, in an intertextual dialogue that was written "out"—simultaneously exposed and erased. Because supporters of the Revolution represented it as an apocalyptic event that would transform the world, they read and wrote the Revolution as an original break from the "terms" of the

142

past, and their representation became a dominant paradigm in the subsequent postrevolutionary historiography. In my essay, I trace some key intertextual dialogues radicals were reproducing in their promotion of new knowledge and discoveries through the tradition they were writing within. I then focus on the intertextual war between Edmund Burke and the writers opposing him— Thomas Paine, Mary Wollstonecraft, Helen Maria Williams, and James Mackintosh—concentrating on Mackintosh's response to Burke by which he changed the terms of the debate from tradition versus discovery to a revolution embodying both. I illustrate how both sides were reinscribing an old debate into the seemingly new language of the French Revolution. Since I explore a series of intertextual repetitions and resemblances, Karl Marx's well-known comments at the beginning of the *Eighteenth Brumaire of Louis Bonaparte* (1852) on the tendency of revolutionaries to represent themselves in the repetitive language of a radical tradition provides an appropriate prelude to the theme of light and knowledge emanating from the writers of 1789.

I

Throughout the 1790s, the Anglo-American supporters commonly referred to the Revolution as a liberating light, dispelling the obscurant darkness of the old "Gothic" order. This, in turn, had been an imagistic commonplace of Enlightenment writers in their war against tradition and the *infâme*. Light was inevitably progressive. In 1684 Pierre Bayle, in article 11 of *Nouvelles de la république des lettres,* had repeated a sentiment that would be reinscribed by radical writers in the 1790s: "We are now in an age which bids fair to become more and more enlightened, so much so that all preceding ages when compared with this will seem plunged into darkness." The Enlightenment commonplace was also a commonplace of Renaissance humanists who had "invented the concept of the 'middle' ages—which they also thought of as the 'dark' ages"—and which they contrasted to the new era of epistemological light.[1] The fact that the ideological opposition of darkness and light was biblically derivative further enmeshed rebellious readers of tradition in the repetitive texts of history.[2]

In the 1790s, light and darkness were, again, antithetic metaphors for liberating knowledge and oppressive ignorance, and the former was opposed to traditional religious warnings against dangerous knowledge. But this contrast had a history of its own.

In *An Essay Concerning Human Understanding* (1690), John Locke, for instance, criticized the man who, in search of "mathematical truths . . . stopped his thoughts short and went not so far": "The same thing may happen concerning the notions we have of the being of a Deity. For, though there be no truth which a man may more evidently make out to himself than the existence of a God, yet he that shall content himself with things as he finds them in this world . . . and not make inquiry a little further into their causes, ends, and admirable contrivances . . . may live long without any notions of such a Being."[3]

Locke was responding to a variety of traditional texts enjoining epistemological restraint, such as the first book of Richard Hooker's *Of the Laws of Ecclesiastical Polity* (1593):

> Dangerous it were for the feeble brain of man to wade far into the doings of the most High, whom although to know be life, and joy to make mention of his name: yet our soundest knowledge is to know that we know him not as in deed he is, neither can we know him: and our safest eloquence concerning him is our silence, when we confess without confession that his glory is inexplicable, his greatness above our capacity and reach. He is above, and we upon earth, therefore it behoveth our words to be wary and few.[4]

Two centuries later, in the debate over the French Revolution, Mary Wollstonecraft repeated Locke's critique of Hooker's prohibitive ignorance of "the most High." In *A Vindication of the Rights of Woman* (1792), Wollstonecraft disclaims "that specious humility which, after investigating nature, stops at the author.—The High and Lofty one, who inhabiteth eternity, doubtless possesses many attributes of which we can form no conception, but reason tells me that they cannot clash with those I adore—and I am compelled to listen to her voice."[5] Wollstonecraft dares to go farther, but affirms her intellectual independence in the adopted language of prior epistemological exploration, reinscribing her rebellious reading in context of a textual "other" that she writes "out."

In repeating radical tradition, revolutionaries imagined they were writing within a different representational system than their antirevolutionary enemies, but, to return to Marx, they were not merely repeating radical tradition, they were repeating the rebellious representations of conservative tradition. The rebellion against the traditional canon, for instance, involved a rebellious reading of canonical texts that had celebrated epistemological restraint and hierarchic distinction. Radicals in the 1790s posed as ur-rebels, recreating an allegory of forbidden knowledge, miming

Satan's ur-rebellion, and prefiguring other Romantic rebellions in the nineteenth century. In deconstructing the contradictions and distinctions of the counterrevolutionary world, they acted out their rebellions in the terms of "counterrevolutionary" tradition. Revolutionary deconstruction contained the seeds of its own reconstruction: in texts which identify with subversive inversion, in which traditional good is evil and vice versa, where rebellion is represented as liberation from repression, and knowledge is the forbidden fruit that sets people free—writers wrote out their revolutions in the mimetic terms of the past.

Because they wrote within and "out" of the same textual tradition, radical writers in the 1790s shared the same preoccupations with models and copies, origins and originality that earlier writers had expressed in their own war against tradition and authority. For all these writers, knowledge was the liberating paradigm of human freedom and its discovery the genesis of world regeneration. There was hence a historical intertextual background for the ideological wars of Locke, Wollstonecraft, and the other eighteenth-century writers who were advocating an epistemological revolution.

Like their ideological predecessors, the writers who promoted the French Revolution had a great faith in the discovery of principles that would ensure human progress. The language of discovery had a special resonance in the revolutionary era and had been echoed earlier in the Enlightenment. In both eras, the theme of discovery was often in the context of revealed knowledge (hidden or suppressed by the old, oppressive order) and in countercontext to Genesis and forbidden knowledge. The latter, of course, had been the dominant paradigm for centuries: the Church had incessantly warned against epistemological lust and arrogance. Saint Bonaventure (1221–1274), for instance, had opposed a heterodox (and misunderstood) form of Aristotelianism (that there were a multiplicity of truths and realities) being taught in the University of Paris, comparing this mutant form of "Aristotelian" philosophy to the forbidden tree of knowledge: "if you eat from this *tree of knowledge of good and evil,* you fall away from the faith."[6]

Carlo Ginzburg provides another epistemological context, Saint Paul's Epistle to the Romans (11:20) against moral pride had been imprecisely translated from Greek to Latin *(noli altum sapere, sed time)* in Jerome's Vulgate and was, after the fourth century, consequently misunderstood in the Latin West: "'*Sapere*' was taken not as a verb with a moral meaning ('to know') . . . In this way St. Paul's condemnation of moral pride became a warning against intellectual curiosity." Paul's admonition was consequently understood as a warning against philosophical and theological speculation—heretical "forbidden knowledge"—and hence had political and religious implications. Although various commentators, including Erasmus, noted that Paul's text had been misunderstood, the misunderstanding stood, appearing in Western texts and emblem books for centuries.[7]

The advent of the new science, however, changed the traditional formulation. The conventional symbols of arrogance and pride—Icarus and Prometheus who had broken sacred taboos and had fallen—"became symbols of a powerful intellectual drive towards discovery. In a dramatic shift of values, 'boldness,' 'curiosity,' and 'intellectual pride'—vices traditionally associated with the myths—were now seen as virtues."[8] Conservatives, not surprisingly, counterattacked with the traditional biblical paradigms. Reacting against what he saw as the intellectual arrogance and the materialist bent of those associated with the new science, Henry More, writing in 1648, worried about the spiritual consequence of the new knowledge: "Till men as eagerly seek after temperance and modesty," their intellectual explorations seemed to him "like the building of Babel . . . the ground work of Luciferan knowledge."[9]

In their correspondent critiques, both sides reinscribed each other's language and paradigms. At the beginning of the *Advancement of Learning* (1605), Francis Bacon, for instance, reformulates the traditional critique of knowledge, which he criticizes and rejects:

> Knowledge is of those things which are to be accepted of with great limitation and caution; that the aspiring to over-much knowledge as the original temptation and sin, whereupon ensued the fall of man; that knowledge hath in it somewhat of the serpent and therefore where it entereth into a man it makes him swell . . . that experience demonstrates how learned men have been arch-heretics, how learned times have been inclined to atheism, and how the contemplation of second causes doth derogate from our dependence upon God, who is the first cause.[10]

But the new revolution in knowledge, albeit resisted, eventually swept aside the old epistemological parables and paradigms. Seventeenth-century emblem books consequently stressed boldness and discovery—to dare everything—themes rearticulated by Enlightenment and revolutionary writers. A phrase from Horace's *Epistle to Lollius* ("sapere aude," literally "dare to be wise") came to mean "Dare to know" and was affixed to emblem books that had once borne Saint Paul's admonitory injunction.[11] There was a thematic revolution and a shift from a parable of forbidden knowledge to the liberating knowledge that sets people free. In his 1784 essay, "What Is Enlightenment?" Kant replies that it is man's emergence from self-imposed nonage and challenges people to begin liberating themselves by acquiring knowledge instead of relying on tradition: "Dare to know! *(Sapere aude.)* 'Have the courage to use your understanding' is therefore the motto of the enlightenment."[12] Saint Paul's mistranslated *sapere* had come full circle.

Robert Darnton provides another context for this epistemological shift. In "Philosophers Trim the Tree of Knowledge," chapter five of *The Great Cat Massacre,* Darnton illustrates that the *philosophes* contributing to Diderot's *Encyclopédie* engaged in a reorganization of traditional epistemological boundaries, challenging and replacing the conventional emphasis on theology in traditional diagrams of the tree of knowledge with the *philosophe*—the bearer of enlightenment in the modern world.[13]

Enlightenment writers reformulated the parable of forbidden knowledge: oppressive kings and priests had conspired to prohibit knowledge to keep people mystified and oppressed.[14] In the *Encyclopédie,* for instance, "enlightenment," as reasoned knowledge, "was directly opposed to all knowledge transmitted or authorized . . . by the Church." Diderot contrasted an "'enlightened century' to 'times of darkness and ignorance.'" Voltaire suggested that "'a Gothic government snuffed out all enlightenment; for almost 1200 years.'"[15] This Enlightenment critique reappeared in the revolutionary critique. In the *Prospect Papers* (1804), Thomas Paine repeated radical tradition: "Reason is the forbidden tree of priestcraft and may serve to explain the allegory of the forbidden tree of knowledge, for we may reasonably suppose the allegory had some meaning and application at the time it was invented."[16]

In the 1790s, revolutionaries also waged an intertextual war against a conservative canon that emphasized epistemological boundaries and restraint. In England this canon consisted of the Bible and, *inter alia,* works by Milton, Pope, Johnson, and Burke—the traditional authoritative documents of the old order.[17] Blake's subversive reading of *Paradise Lost* is well known; in *A Vindication of the Rights of Woman* (1792), Mary Wollstonecraft also engaged in an elaborate subversive reading, identifying with Satan and questioning the numerous condemnations of epistemological appetite by Raphael and others. She brilliantly reinscribed Satan's subversive questioning of God's prohibition of "knowledge": Why has God prohibited Adam and Eve from eating from the "forbidden" tree of knowledge—"Why but to awe, / Why but to keep ye low and ignorant, / His worshippers" (*Paradise Lost* 9.703–05). This was, of course, the answer provided by *philosophes* and revolutionaries criticizing priestcraft and monarchy (cf. Locke, *Essay,* 4.20.4), and, in Wollstonecraft's case, patriarchy.[18] In *An Historical and Moral View of the French Revolution* (1794), Wollstonecraft added this coda: "We must get entirely clear of all notions drawn from the wild traditions of original sin: the eating of the apple, the theft of Prometheus, the opening of Pandora's box, and other fables, too tedious to enumerate, on which priests have erected their tremendous structures of imposition, to persuade us, that we are naturally inclined to evil."[19]

In the endeavor to rewrite this tradition, reason, knowledge, and discovery were incantatory talismans in the revolutionary litany: light and liberation proceed from revelation, the discovery of new or forbidden knowledge. The themes and metaphors of discovery—the exploration of new worlds, the celebrated intellectual voyages of the world's philosophic liberators, the bearers of enlightenment—these themes and metaphors link the Enlightenment to the revolutionary and Romantic eras—all the brave discoverers who dared to know—valiant voyagers who were the first to burst upon that silent sea.[20]

For James Mackintosh (1765–1832), Bacon and Locke were such daring discoverers and hence he and other advocates of the Revolution wrote "out" radical tradition through the "new" paradigms of knowledge and discovery. In fact, the language and themes of Bacon's *Magna instauratio* (1620) reappeared in the radical texts of the 1790s and were contested by writers like Burke, who insisted that there were "no discoveries" to be made in morality and politics.[21] In *Magna instauratio,* Bacon had commenced a new restoration of the foundations of knowledge and a correspondent critique of traditional (scholastic) knowledge, copied in "endless repetitions." He noted the error of confusing the advancement of knowledge with the parable of forbidden knowledge. In contrast, he promoted "new discoveries"; indeed, *discovery* is the primary thematic word of his work; at one point, he compares himself with Columbus, who, "before that wonderful voyage . . . across the Atlantic . . . gave the reasons of his conviction that new lands and continents might be discovered besides those which were known before." Considering it an intellectual disgrace that, in an age of celebrated physical discoveries, "the intellectual globe should remain shut up and within the narrow limits of old discoveries," Bacon insisted on the courage to go beyond previous repetitious boundaries:

> We have no reason to be ashamed of the [ancient] discoveries which have been made . . . but as in former ages when men sailed only by observation of the stars, they could indeed coast along the shores of the old continent or cross a few small and mediterranean seas, but before the ocean could be traversed and the new world discovered, the use of the mariner's needle, as a more faithful and certain guide, had to be found out; in like manner the discoveries which have been hitherto made in the arts and sciences [have been based superficially on "near" human senses and "common notions"]; but before we can reach the remoter and more hidden parts of nature, it is necessary that a more perfect use and application of the human mind and intellect be introduced.[22]

Likewise, in *An Essay Concerning Human Understanding*, Locke, a close reader of Bacon, refers to "new discoveries" (an iconoclastic phrase with a long tradition) he had made and encourages us to seek and extend knowledge, employing reason, the light that shines within to make "discoveries."[23] Throughout the later part of the *Essay, discovery* means the detection of truth, and Locke encourages the intellectual search for "new discoveries" concerning human knowledge.[24] He condemns repetitive "beaten tracks . . . whose thoughts reach only to imitation," and is "bold to say" that there are extraordinary men who could, in the seventeenth century, "open new and undiscovered ways to the advancement of knowledge" (4.17.7; note the closing allusion to Bacon). In an essay on Bacon and Locke, James Mackintosh praises the latter for exhorting "posterity to push their conquests to its upmost verge, with a boldness which will be fully justified only by the discoveries of ages from which we are yet far distant."[25]

In the *Reflections,* Edmund Burke, in contrast, had dismissed the language of discovery employed by *philosophes* and revolutionaries:

> [w]e know that *we* [Burke and the English people] have made no discoveries; and we think that no discoveries are to be made in morality; nor many in the great principles of government, nor in the ideas of liberty, which were understood long before we were born, altogether as well as they will be after the grave has heaped its mould upon our presumption, and the silent tomb shall have imposed its law on our pert loquacity. (182)

Burke appropriately alludes to the classical conception of political change, given by Aristotle, who had, in book seven of *The Politics,* formulated its canonical expression. For Aristotle, there can be no new beginning, since practically everything had been "in the course of ages discovered many times over, or rather infinitely often."[26] Revolutionaries, in contrast, "place all their hopes in discovery" (*R*, 184). Richard Price, the radical promoter of the French Revolution, "talks as if he had made a discovery," but "only follows a precedent" (*R*, 158). In order to indict an entire corporate order, revolutionaries ransack the past for evil examples and "delight in the investigation of such discoveries" (*R*, 254). They enjoy stigmatizing and degrading the nobles and clergy, but Burke is "not sagacious enough to discover how this despotic sport" differs from "the rankest tyranny" (*R*, 266). The irony is, for Burke, that revolutionaries talk of discovery but only repeat the tyrannical history and precedents of the past, ironically validating the Burkean Aristotelian point that there are no discoveries (even evil discoveries) to be made: "They proceed exactly as their ancestors of ambition have done before them . . . nothing at all . . . is new. They follow precedents and examples . . . they never depart an iota from the authentic formulas of tyranny and usurpation" (*R*, 277). Burke can only examine what the revolutionaries have done in order to "discover" if their endeavors "justify these bold undertakers in the superiority which they assume over mankind" (*R*, 284). Both Burke and his respondents use the verb *discover* in the sense "to shew; to disclose; to bring to light . . . . To make known" and hence to reveal—definitions 1 and 2 in Samuel Johnson's *Dictionary* (1755).

Burke's opponents countered in the "other" language of discovery, reemphasizing it in their responses. Paine, for instance, in *Rights of Man* (1791), argued that the American Revolution "led to a discovery of the principles" of society and the rights of man,[27] and he presented himself as the ur-discoverer of both the principles and the knowledge that would set people free. In her *Letters from France* (1790), Helen Maria Williams, responding to Burke, is thankful that she lives in such an "enlightened period" and that "the human mind has made as many important discoveries in morality as in science"; she believes the French revolutionaries had ventured on a bold exploration and that it is "within the compass of human ability to form a system of politics, which like a modern ship of discovery" sails "sublimely over the untracked ocean," establishing "a line of connection across the divided world."[28]

In *Vindiciae gallicae* (1791), one of James Mackintosh's prerevolutionary heroes is A.-R.-J. Turgot, who "preferred nothing to the discovery of truth" (*WJM*, 407). The "great works" of the *philosophes* contain moral and political "discoveries" (424). Contra Montesquieu, Mackintosh notes the fact that a representative democracy can function harmoniously in a large country was a "great discovery" (441). He refers to the National Assembly and "a new aera of history": "It was time . . . that legislators . . . should, guided by the *polarity* of reason, hazard a bolder navigation, and discover, in unexplored regions, the treasure of public felicity." In such a time, bold navigation replaces "the narrow and dastardly *coasting* which never ventures to lose sight of usage and precedent" (423).[29]

Mackintosh, however, has it both ways, subsequently arguing in *Vindiciae* that the French National Assembly did not, in fact, discover new truths and principles but was rearticulating what had been discovered by the Americans: "To the juvenile vigour of reason and freedom in the New World—where the human mind was unencumbered with the vast mass of usage and prejudice, which so many ages of ignorance had accumulated, to load and deform society in Europe—France owed . . . lessons" (*WJM*, 438–39). This was a popular thesis pushed by Paine and others.

Since the French were simply implementing new-world discoveries, Mackintosh argues, Burke was egregiously wrong to argue that they had overthrown all established precedents. The "French legislators," likewise, had merely installed the Enlightenment: "the conviction of a great majority of Enlightened men" that had, over a century, "become on most questions of general politics, uniform." The "National Assembly was therefore not called on to make discoveries" (*WJM*, 423). Mackintosh ironically reformulates Burke's contention in the *Reflections* that there were "no discoveries . . . to be made." Since, according to Mackintosh, "all the great questions of general politics" had already "been nearly decided," it did not matter that the great Enlightenment "works in which discoveries are contained" were not read by the common people, because the Enlightenment trickled down to the people, once the discoveries became the common linguistic currency that had been used by "the reflecting few" (*WJM*, 423, 424).

Expanding on a point made by Helen Maria Williams,[30] Mackintosh compares politics to science: discovered principles and laws can be changed from theory into practical reality, just as a mechanic who had mathematically proved that by altering "the structure of a machine, its effect would be increased *four-fold*." This mechanic would certainly not (as Europe previously had—ignoring the discovered principles of the Enlightenment) refuse to implement the alteration merely because he had been the first to discover the mathematical equation or law. Thus "geometry . . . bears nearly the same relation to mechanics that abstract reasoning does to politics" (*WJM*, 423). Mackintosh reiterates the tradition of seventeenth-century Cartesian rationalism and the predilection for mechanical, mathematical models, supposedly by which political and social principles can be discovered to be as true and precise as a scientific law or a mathematical equation. This was of course a line of argument that Burke had attacked throughout the *Reflections:* the revolutionaries adopt an abstract, reductive "metaphysical" model and impossibly try to force people to fit it. Mackintosh, in the *Vindiciae*, embraces what Burke rejects, reversing Burke's representation—the dangerous, abstract, and impractical theories that do not correspond to reality are actually proven principles (like the principles of Newton and Archimedes) reified by practical experience. Arguing diametrically against Burke, Mackintosh ironically resembles him in his emphasis on rediscovery and his articulation of a practical, "proven" Enlightenment "tradition," sanctified by experience and time. He has it both ways, since he rearticulates principles that had, until recently, been partially suppressed by Despotism. Mackintosh, in contrast to other revolutionary supporters who were reproducing the old paradigms of "new" discovery, rewrote Burke's critique and reinscribed the language of traditional (re)-discovery in his vindication of the French Revolution. His intertextual war with Burke illustrates that both Left and Right, in the 1790s, were self-consciously refighting previous ideological battles as they were revising each other's languages. Mackintosh specifically reiterates and reveals to his benighted English audience the rediscovered principles of revolutionary France, which he hopes will be equally copied in reactionary England.

II

The theme of discovery complements the theme of copies and models that are either venerable and admirable or imitative and derivative. Imitation of the ancients or "nature" had been traditionally extolled, but by the late eighteenth century, originality was privileged over the repetition of models that had lost their relevancy. The lamp was beginning to replace the mirror.[31] Not surprisingly, this theme was also broached by Burke in the *Reflections,* where models and examples are either good or bad: Richard

Price and other revolutionary Dissenters endeavor to seduce the English into an "imitation" of the National Assembly; some French revolutionaries falsely claim that they are only following "the example of England," but the English people abhor the "model" of revolutionary France; Richard Price "talks as if he had made a discovery" but only "repeats" discredited radical discourse; the revolutionaries represent themselves as being original and new but everything they do is imitative—"[t]hey follow [the] precedents and examples" of past tyrants and regicides; they "copy" Cicero's Cato, in endeavoring to found a republic on "school paradoxes"; they are "servile imitators" of Rousseau, but, nevertheless, "appeal to no practice" and "copy . . . no model" when it comes to creating a constitution—a constitution "the very reverse" of England's. Burke contends that people are insane to present the French constitution as an "example for Great Britain"; the "financial proceedings" of French revolutionaries are not based upon practical, proven "tests" but "models of ideal perfection." Previously the French nobility copied "the worst part of the manners of England," a "foolish imitation," and they unfortunately adopted English Enlightenment literature. There is, however, no fundamental "resemblance" between the two countries, neither in their respective revolutions (1688 and 1789) nor in the "reformation" of their respective religions.[32] A person should not destroy, Burke insists, and attempt to rebuild "without having models and patterns of approved utility before his eyes"— "models" the English "had kept alive"—"the ancient principles and models of the old common law of Europe meliorated and adapted to its present state"; he recommends to the French "the example of the British constitution" and hopes his countrymen will not "imitate" French constitutional "models," but rather the wise "caution" of English forefathers.[33]

Mackintosh, in response, turns Burke's "models" and "copies" against him. Alluding to Burke's assertion that Richard Price "talks as if he had made a discovery" but "only follows a precedent" and that revolutionaries do nothing new but follow tyrannical "precedents and examples" (R, 158, 277), Mackintosh, in the *Vindiciae*, revises Burke's representation: the despotic "governors" of the old European order "tyrannize by precedent, and oppress in reverent imitation of models consecrated by the usage of despotic predecessors" (WJM, 437; cf. 455). Mackintosh reduces Burkean reverence for tradition and precedents to the repetitive oppression of despotic predecessors, and he continues subverting Burke's critique. English admirers of the French Revolution do not wish "to imitate it"; they realize that "the conduct of nations" varies with their "circumstances" (an ironic Burkean point). In contrast, "[b]lind admirers of Revolutions take them for implicit models. Thus Mr. Burke admires that of 1689," while English admirers of France look to her Revolution, "not to model our conduct, but to invigorate the spirit of freedom": "We are not bound to copy the conduct of the French revolutionaries . . . Exact imitation is not necessary to reverence" (*WJM*, 457). Mackintosh, in effect, accuses Burke of doing what he accuses English admirers of the French Revolution: slavish imitation of the (1688) Revolution, instead of distinguishing the historical circumstances pertaining to different times and places. In doing this, Mackintosh resembles Burke reprobating revolutionary admirers, while Burke, in Mackintosh's representation, resembles his own copy of revolutionary admirers who wish to imitate revolutionary models, but who follow old, reactionary "precedents."

Indeed, Mackintosh poses as the reforming conservative, warning the English that the French example will be copied if English governors "imitate" the old French government's "policy." This was the same threat issued by Paine in the *Rights of Man:* enact revolutionary reforms or face your own French Revolution.[34] Mackintosh, however, threatens in the mimic role of the Burkean defender of English tradition. Having spent much of the *Vindiciae* denigrating monarchy, corporate orders, and aristocratic distinction, he is suddenly one of the "true friends of order," upholding "the prerogative of the monarchy, the splendour of the hierarchy, and the dignity of the peerage" (*WJM*, 457; the sentence is cast as an affirmative rhetorical question: "Who are the true friends of order . . .")—all which will unfortunately be swept away unless the English institute reforms resembling those of the French Revolution—electoral reform, the abolition of repressive taxes, and the abrogation of laws against Dissenters (455–56). Citing Burke against Burke ("The beginnings of confusion in England are at present feeble enough; but . . . [w]henever our neighbor's [France's] house is on fire, it cannot be amiss for the engines to play a little upon our own," *R*, 92), Mackintosh becomes the ironic Burkean defender of order, prophetically warning of revolutionary disorders in England: "This language, taken in its most natural sense, is exactly what the friends of Reform in England would adopt" (*WJM* 457). "Such are the sentiments of those who can admire without servilely copying recent changes, and can venerate the principles without superstitiously defending the corrupt reliques of old revolutions" (457).

The contrast between Burke, the servile copier of the past, and his vindication of the "new" French Revolution mimes Burke's critique of revolutionary imitators in the *Reflections*, illustrating again how both the Left and Right in the 1790s were refighting previous ideological battles dealing with authority and innovation in an ongoing battle over old books and texts. Mackintosh and Burke additionally illustrate how both Left and Right continually reabsorbed each other, even as they wrote the other "out," suggesting how these intertextual wars have continued to be reabsorbed into the Revolution's ongoing historiography.

In retrospect, writers in the 1790s were reabsorbing and translating the terms of previous paradigms into the ongoing text of the French Revolution. Writing in and out of the same system of representation, both opponents and advocates of the Revolution told similar, albeit disguised, stories in a variety of texts whose secret signatures and traces constituted a complementary intertextual palimpsest. Preoccupied with a true source and illegitimate copies, radical writers reinscribed the old battles over authority and innovation, discovery and imitation, in the seemingly new language of revolution and apocalypse. Radical writers reinscribed a neo-Platonic critique of tradition, in which counter-revolution was based on a debased, illegitimate "copy," removed from a true, epistemological source. Consequently, the terms of both radical and conservative critiques often reflected each other. In *The Order of Things*, Michel Foucault discusses a "classical" *episteme* based on correspondence and identity, in which signifier and signified are one, and a moden *episteme* of discrepancy and difference which displaces the earlier paradigm.[35] These two *epistemes* were crucial in the writing out of the Revolution's history, for it made the French Revolution familiar by repeating an old myth— the fall from unity into fragmentation and the promise of reintegration in the future. The old myth of the Fall was rewritten as the new myth of revolution, and illusion and reality, that obsessive theme of Western metaphysics, corresponded to a system of complementary differences drawing their defining identity from the "other." That the historiography of revolution of the past two centuries has repeated the paradigms reformulated by writers in the 1790s suggests that while an anxiety of influence can be paradoxically reassuring, an event as complex as the French Revolution can only be written as a familiar, recognizable story.[36]

Notes

1. Quentin Skinner, *The Foundations of Modern Political Thought*, 2 vols. (Cambridge: Cambridge University Press, 1978), 1:110.

2. See Ronald Paulson, *Representations of Revolution, 1789–1820* (New Haven: Yale University Press, 1983), 46–47.

3. John Locke, *An Essay Concerning Human Understanding*, 1.3.23.

4. Richard Hooker, *Of the Laws of Ecclesiastical Polity*, ed. Arthur Stephen McGrade (Cambridge: Cambridge University Press, 1989), 55. Hooker, in turn, was responding to John Calvin, *Institutes of the Christian Religion* (1559). In book 1, chapter 16, Calvin reprobates the "carnal mind," which "once it has perceived the power of God in creation, stops there . . . But faith must penetrate deeper." See *Institutes of the Christian Religion*, trans. Henry Beveridge (Grand Rapids, Mich.: Eerdman, 1989), 172.

5. *The Works of Mary Wollstonecraft*, ed. Janet Todd and Marilyn Butler, 7 vols. (New York: New York University Press, 1989), 5: 115.

6. Saint Bonaventure, *The Tree of Life*, trans. Ewert Cousins (New York: Paulist Press, 1978), 11; Paul A. Rahe, *Republics Ancient and Modern: Classical Republicanism and the American Revolution* (Chapel Hill: University of North Carolina Press, 1992), 228.

7. Carlo Ginzburg, "High and Low: The Theme of Forbidden Knowledge in the Sixteenth and Seventeenth Centuries," *Past and Present* 73 (1976): 28–29.

8. Ibid., 38.

9. Quoted by Rahe, *Republics Ancient and Modern*, 365.

10. Francis Bacon, *Essays, Advancement of Learning, New Atlantis, and Other Pieces*, ed. Richard Foster Jones (New York: Odyssey Press, 1937), 174–75.

11. Ginzburg, "High and Low," 40.

12. Immanuel Kant, "What Is Enlightenment?" in *The Enlightenment: A Comprehensive Anthology*, ed. and trans. Peter Gay (New York: Simon & Schuster, 1973), 384.

13. Robert Darnton, *The Great Cat Massacre and Other Episodes in French Cultural History* (New York: Random House, 1984), 191–209.

14. Another ideological context is the Protestant Reformation and the emphasis on the printing press and vernacular Bibles that could be read by the people—people formerly controlled and mystified by the institutional readings of the "Latin" Church. There are important links between the Reformation, the Enlightenment, and the Revolution.

15. Marie-Hélène Huet, "Thunder and Revolution: Franklin, Robespierre, Sade," in *The French Revolution (1789–1989): Two Hundred Years of Rethinking*, ed. Sandy Petrey (Lubbock: Texas Tech University Press, 1989), 18.

16. *The Complete Writings of Thomas Paine*, ed. Philip S. Foner, 2 vols. (New York: Citadel Press, 1945), 2: 800.

17. Not all revolutionaries, of course, attacked the Bible and Milton, for both were also used to valorize the Revolution. My discussion is in context of the debate over knowledge and discovery, which is simultaneously a debate over the Revolution's meaning. In *Reflections on the Revolution in France* (1790) and other antirevolutionary writings, Edmund Burke saw the Revolution as a second "Fall" into an obsessive knowledge of evil. See Steven Blakemore, *Burke and the Fall of Language: The French Revolution as Linguistic Event* (Hanover, N.H.: University Press of New England, 1988), 61–76.

18. See Steven Blakemore, "Rebellious Reading: The Doubleness of Wollstonecraft's Subversion of *Paradise Lost*," *Texas Studies in Literature and Language* 34 (1992): 451–80.

19. Wollstonecraft, *Works*, 6: 21–22.

20. There was a respondent conservative language of discovery which ironically mimed its radical counterpart, but which stressed matchless discoveries originating in the past. In his fifteenth and last *Discourse* on painting (December 1790), Sir Joshua Reynolds extolled Michelangelo's sublime imagination, contrasting his art with the imitative art of subsequent, inferior artists: Michelangelo possessed "the same daring spirit, which urged him first to explore the unknown regions of the imagination, delighted with the novelty, and animated by the success of his discoveries, could not have failed to stimulate and impel

him forward in his career beyond those limits, which his followers, destitute of the same incentives, had not strength to pass. . . . In pursuing this great Art, it must be acknowledged that we labour under greater difficulties than those who were born in the age of its discovery, and whose minds from their infancy were habituated to this style; who learnt it as language, as their mother tongue." Sir Joshua Reynolds, *Discourses on Art,* ed. Robert R. Wark (New Haven: Yale University Press, 1975), 272, 278.

21. Edmund Burke, *Reflections on the Revolution in France,* ed. Conor Cruise O'Brien (Harmondsworth: Penguin Books, 1986), 182; hereafter *R,* cited in the text.

22. Bacon, *Essay,* 401, 403, 425, 445, 462.

23. Locke, *Essay Concerning Human Understanding,* "Epistle," par. 5; "Introduction," par. 5; cf. 4.3.6, 4.7.11.

24. Ibid., 4.17.6–7; 4.17.10; 4.20.4; 4.21.5.

25. *The Miscellaneous Works of the Right Honourable Sir James Mackintosh* (New York: Appleton, 1870), 18; hereafter *WJM,* cited in the text.

26. Aristotle, *The Politics,* trans. T. A. Sinclair (Harmondsworth: Penguin Books, 1962), 419; see also 7.1329b, 25–30.

27. Paine, *Writings,* 1: 360.

28. Helen Maria Williams, *Letters from France,* ed. Janet M. Todd, 2 vols. (Delmar, N.Y.: Scholars' Facsimiles & Reprints, 1975), 1: 65, 222.

29. Cf. Bacon, *Magna instauratio,* 248, 253–54).

30. Williams, *Letters,* 1:220–22.

31. In *Conjectures on Original Composition* (1759), Edward Young provided the classic eighteenth-century rereading of textual "tradition" as derivative, imitative "copies."

32. Burke, *Reflections,* 91, 158, 184, 185, 277, 283, 304, 353, 244, 258.

33. Ibid., 123, 152, 375, 376. In France, the Abbé Sieyès (who Burke is possibly arguing against; see *Reflections,* 118) criticized those Frenchmen who wanted to imitate England's constitution. Section four of chapter four of *What Is the Third Estate?* (1789) is titled "A spirit of imitation is not a fit guide for us." Those who want to imitate the English constitution are either the young or the old: "The young try to copy; the old but can repeat." The English constitution is defective and "if ideal models of the beautiful and good exist [cf. Burke: the English have "models and patterns of approved utility," *Reflections,* 152] . . . how then can we disregard the true good and be satisfied with imitating its copy?" Joseph Emmanuel Sieyès, *What Is the Third Estate?* trans. M. Blondel (New York: Praeger, 1964), 117. Note the Platonic vocabulary. In the National Assembly (1789–90), French "imitation" of England was also ridiculed and criticized. Jean-Joseph Mounier and the *Monarchiens* were given short shrift.

34. Paine, *Writings,* 1: 353, 450–51.

35. Michel Foucault, *The Order of Things: An Archeology of the Human Sciences,* trans. A. M. Sheridan Smith (New York: Vintage Books, 1973), chaps. 2 and 3.

36. Gilles Deleuze, in *Difference and Repetition,* trans. Paul Patton (New York: Columbia University Press, 1994), explores the problems and limits of Western representation of the "other."